Although this book will make yo̶ ̶ ̶ ̶ ̶ ̶ ̶ ̶
parenting light. It's filled with tru̶ ̶ ̶ ̶ ̶ ̶ ̶ ̶ ̶ ̶ ̶ your home
for good. I love that it's intensely practical. You get the feeling
this father-and-son writing team has spent time observing your
children (how else would they know so much!). Let this dynamic
duo help turn your greatest frustrations in parenting into your
greatest victories.

ARLENE PELLICANE
Speaker and author of *Parents Rising: 8 Strategies for Raising Kids Who Love God, Respect Authority, and Value What's Right*

If you really love your kids, take the time to read this book.
Parenting Is Hard and Then You Die is a great combination of
humor and Bible-based wisdom. Dr. Clarke's personal approach
and creative strategies will help you raise healthy kids who love you
and love the Lord.

DAVID AND CLAUDIA ARP
Cofounders of Marriage Alive and authors of *10 Great Dates*

In David Clarke's *Parenting Is Hard and Then You Die*, parents will
find practical guidelines and insights that will change parenting
from an ordeal to be endured to an enriching experience. This
book is full of humor, biblical applications, and just plain common
sense.

HAROLD J. SALA, PH.D.
Author and founder of Guidelines International

Parenting Is Hard and Then You Die is a fun, fun book—you'll
laugh hilariously at your own life. David Clarke is insightful,
practical, and very vulnerable, as well as funny.

JIM CONWAY, PH.D.
President, Midlife Dimensions, and author of *Men in Midlife Crisis*

Parenting Is Hard

and Then You Die

A FUN BUT HONEST LOOK AT RAISING KIDS OF ALL AGES RIGHT

David E. Clarke, Ph.D.
with William G. Clarke, M.A.

TYNDALE HOUSE PUBLISHERS, INC.
CAROL STREAM, ILLINOIS

FOCUS ON THE FAMILY® | FOCUS ON PARENTING™

Parenting Is Hard and Then You Die: A Fun but Honest Look at Raising Kids of All Ages Right
© 2019 David E. Clarke. All rights reserved.

A Focus on the Family book published by Tyndale House Publishers, Inc., Carol Stream, Illinois 60188

Focus on the Family and the accompanying logo and design are federally registered trademarks of Focus on the Family, 8605 Explorer Drive, Colorado Springs, CO 80920.

TYNDALE and Tyndale's quill logo are registered trademarks of Tyndale House Publishers, Inc.

Editors: Larry Weeden and Kathy Davis
Cover design by Nathan Cook

People's names and certain details of their stories have been changed to protect the privacy of the individuals involved. However, the facts of what happened and the underlying principles have been conveyed as accurately as possible.

The use of material from or references to various websites does not imply endorsement of those sites in their entirety. Availability of websites and pages is subject to change without notice.

This author is represented by Hartline Literary Agency.

For information about special discounts for bulk purchases, please contact Tyndale House Publishers at csresponse@tyndale.com, or call 1-800-323-9400.

ISBN 978-1-58997-976-5

Printed in the United States of America

25   24   23   22   21   20   19
7   6   5   4   3   2   1

To the four greatest kids in the world:

Emily

Leeann

Nancy

William

Mom and I love you to infinity and are very proud of you.

Contents

Gifts from God—or Instruments of Slow Torture?

THERE IS ONE QUESTION that has haunted parents for centuries. Here it is: Are children gifts from God—or instruments of slow torture? Actually, they are both. Parenting has moments of wonder, excitement, and enrichment . . . broken up by long stretches of exasperation, total chaos, and suffering.

As you begin parenthood with a newborn baby, you just want this little person to survive. You sneak into the nursery every thirty minutes to make sure the little thing is still breathing. You meet every need of this small, helpless creature.

When your child hits the twos and threes and is systematically destroying your home—piece by broken piece—you begin to wonder if you will survive.

When your child moves into middle school and becomes a teenager, you *know* you're not going to make it. You realize with horror that the roles are reversed. You are now a small, helpless creature at the mercy of a far superior force: hormones.

If you and your ungrateful, hostile, and attitude-challenged teenager survive through high school, two things happen. One, your health is broken. Two, you must now spend your retirement savings on college. Talk about a gamble! All that money for a kid you're not even sure is going to turn out well.

With your health broken and your money spent, you must spend your declining years praying that one of your kids will have pity on you and take care of you. That's the main reason Sandy and I had four kids. We figure at least one of them will look after us when we're in our wheelchair years.

So far, it doesn't look too positive. In a recent conversation with our feisty third daughter, Nancy, the topic of what to do with an aging mom and dad came up. Nancy, deadpan, looked me in the eye and said, "Simple solution. I'm going to put you in a home." And I don't think she was kidding!

This brief overview of the parenting process is tongue-in-cheek. But there is truth to it, isn't there? Parenting is hard. Very, very hard. Just about impossible, really.

If you are raising a child, you are in a war. A war on many fronts.

A War with Your Children

As my overview of the parenting process revealed, you are in a war with your own kids! Don't get me wrong . . . children are blessings from God. They're fun and endlessly entertaining. They enrich us. They give life new meaning. They are the future.

But kids are also selfish, fiendishly inventive, and naturally gravitate to behaviors that are bad for them. They'll fight you at every turn, test your patience to its limit, and may break your heart with poor decisions.

A War with Your Family

It's common to fight with your spouse over how to raise your children. You have different family backgrounds, different personalities, different parenting styles, different standards of behavior, and different ideas of discipline.

If your spouse becomes your ex-spouse, the war over how to raise your children really heats up. Now there are two different homes with two different sets of rules. If you remarry, these new spouses bring in their own ideas about parenting.

To make the war even more intense, all the leftover pain of the divorce transfers into the parenting process.

Other relatives—grandparents, uncles, aunts, cousins—can also interfere with your ability to raise your children in a consistent, godly way.

A War with the Culture

Satan is hard at work every hour of every day trying to damage your children. He's good at what he does. Very good. Look at how successful Satan has been:

- profanity and nudity on television
- the explosion of accessible pornography on the internet
- social media replacing real communication and real relationships
- the decriminalization of harmful drugs
- homosexual marriage legalized
- bisexuality approved
- transgender individuals applauded
- sex outside marriage normalized and promoted
- living together taking the place of marriage
- no-fault divorce laws
- no prayer and no discipline in public schools

Satan is a master of making sin appear incredibly attractive. It's what he does. His main target audience? Your kids.

It's a crazy world and it's getting crazier—and more sinful—every day.

Okay, that's the bad news. It's true, and it's very bad. But I have good news for you. Very good news.

Parents Make the Difference

Fighting the parenting war on all these fronts can make you feel discouraged and even make you want to give up in despair. It's easy to believe that we are weak and powerless as parents. But that is not true!

My fellow parents, listen to me. We can do a lot as parents. The truth is, we do make the difference in the lives of our children. We have the power and the authority, from God Himself, to influence how our children turn out as adults. Don't just take my word for it. Listen to what God says in Proverbs 22:6: "Train up a child in the way he should go; even when he is old he will not depart from it."

There are two central truths in this verse I want to highlight. First, God is saying that parents can raise healthy kids. We can do it! We can train our children to grow up and live as wise, godly adults.

Second, and very importantly, God is saying that to produce a great kid you must follow a plan. You must have a clear and proper course of action. You don't hope for the best. You purposefully carry out your parenting plan. And, most of the time, your children will turn out beautifully.

A Battle Plan That Works!

What you need, my fellow parents, is a parenting battle plan. A practical, carefully researched, and Bible-based plan. A plan that has been proven to work. It just so happens, I have such a plan.

What you'll read in this book is the way my parents (William and Kathleen) raised my brother, Mark—who is a pastor and a school-teacher—and me. So far, we've turned out pretty well.

My dad, William Clarke, is my writing partner. And my mentor.

And a source of godly, biblical wisdom. It's like writing a book with Moses. He's been married to my mom for over sixty years. He is a master's level marriage and family therapist who's been helping parents and their children for . . . well, forever.

This is the way Sandy—my beautiful wife of thirty-five years—and I raised our four children: Emily, Leeann, Nancy, and William. We've had struggles along the way, but we've stayed the course. They have turned into wonderful, productive, and godly young adults.

So far (hint, hint), we have three grandchildren: Chaz and Emily's Izzy (six) and Andrew and Leeann's Jackie (two) and Tyler (three months). As we support these parents, we're using our time-tested battle strategy.

It's the way I've taught thousands of parents, in my therapy office in Tampa and in my seminars, to raise their kids. As a clinical psychologist, I've worked with parents and their kids for over thirty years. Believe me, I've learned a great deal about parenting in my career.

My parenting Battle Plan isn't perfect. It does not contain all the truth in the universe about parenting. It just works.

Who Ought to Read This Book?

If you are in any kind of parenting or quasi-parenting role, this book is for you:

- biological parent in a traditional family
- single parent
- blended parent family
- adoptive parent
- foster parent
- grandparent
- teacher (at a church or in a school)
- coach
- youth pastor

If you are in one of these roles, God wants to use you to positively influence the children in your care. My parenting principles can help you do that.

My Battle Plan

My Battle Plan has five parts:

Foundation: How to form your parenting team
Needs: How to meet the five critical needs in the life of every child
Discipline: How to create a behavior-based system of standards, rewards, and consequences
Teens: How to deal with the six (finally, not five of something!) massive changes every teenager goes through
Blended: How to heal from the loss of one family and build a new, healthy one

If you follow my Battle Plan, you can win the parenting war. You can raise healthy kids in this crazy world. Kids with God-centered self-esteem. Kids who are responsible, independent, and able to develop good relationships. Kids who will be great friends of yours as adults. Kids who will impact the culture—and not the other way around.

Most importantly, kids who will love Jesus Christ and serve Him.

One gentle warning about my sense of humor: At times, I can be edgy, sarcastic, and over the top. But it's all in good fun. My humor is intended to help you understand and apply my parenting principles.

I love my four kids, and I loved raising them. I want you to have the same positive experience Sandy and I did. Parenting is both very difficult and incredibly joyful. I hope my humor and direct, honest writing style get you through the hard times and help you enjoy the great times.

Now read and answer the following questions to begin your Battle Plan briefing from General David Clarke.

YOUR BATTLE PLAN

1. In what areas are you struggling as a parent?

2. Who or what are you battling in your attempt to raise godly, healthy kids?

    - Your spouse?
    - Your ex-spouse?
    - Other family members?
    - The culture?
    - Your kids?

3. In what areas are your children doing well? In what areas are they not doing well?

4. What are your goals for each of your children?

PART ONE

Foundation

CHAPTER I

YOUR SUPERNATURAL TEAM MEMBER

DO NOT EVER sell a house. Do not buy a house. I'm serious. If you live in a pup tent next to a nuclear waste dump, stay there. It will be easier and better for your health than selling your house and buying a new one.

If you have ever sold a house and bought another one, you know what I'm talking about. "Living nightmare" doesn't even come close to describing the process.

My lovely blonde wife, Sandy, and I spent the last seven months selling our home of thirty-one years and purchasing another home. We're still in recovery.

Throwing out all the useless stuff we'd accumulated over three decades was exhausting. And a little embarrassing. Getting our house ready to sell was expensive. Keeping it cleaned and staged for showings was incredibly annoying. Searching and searching and searching for a new house was unbelievably frustrating. Packing up all the things we were taking was a brutal, never-ending job. I have decided to invest heavily in cardboard box manufacturers.

But the worst part of the miserable experience was dealing with the bank that finally . . . finally . . . finally decided to give us a mortgage loan.

I thought torture was illegal. It's not. Our wonderful bank forced us to reveal every penny we made and every penny we spent in our thirty-five-year marriage. Entire forests were cut down to provide the thousands of forms we signed. More forests were cut down to replace the signed forms that our bank misplaced. After inflicting the maximum amount of pain and suffering possible, our bank—two days before our closing—approved the loan.

As you can see, I could go on and on. I'll end with the two things I told Sandy as we drove away from our closing. First, I apologized for making fun of persons who need an emotional support animal. I get it now. I need at least three emotional support animals.

Second, and most important, I made it clear that I will die in our new home. Emergency responders or funeral home employees—I don't care which—will carry me out in a bag. Because . . . I'm never selling this house.

I feel better after my real estate rant. It's good to get the feelings out. But the real point of my sad story is that you can't sell a house and buy another house on your own. It takes a team to get it all done. I had Sandy. I had our four adult kids. I had my parents. I had Bob and Pam Johns, our best friends. I had Liz Menendez, our wonderful Realtor. And I had God, who got us through every twist and turn of the experience.

It Takes a Team to Parent

Just as you shouldn't sell or buy a home on your own (while you can, it's not advisable), you can't be a successful parent on your own. Parenting is too hard. Too stressful. Too demanding. Too complicated. It's too much of everything to tackle without a team.

In this chapter and the next, I will introduce you to your winning Parenting Team. This team will give you the spiritual, emotional, and practical help you need to get the parenting job done right.

Without God, Forget About It

Your most important team member is God. There's no question about it. I can't even imagine attempting to raise children without God's help. Sandy and I barely made it through parenting four kids *with* His help.

To be a successful parent, you must have these qualities: Love. Respect. Kindness. Compassion. Patience. Wisdom. Forgiveness. Insight. Intuition. Emotional strength. The ability to listen. Communication skills. Self-control. (A lot of self-control.) Understanding. Boundaries. Tolerance. Organization. Acceptance of rejection. Unselfishness. Generosity. The ability to speak the truth in love. Grace.

And this isn't a complete list!

Do you possess all these qualities? Of course not. I don't. Sandy doesn't. No one does.

Who does? God does. When you have a relationship with God, you have full access to Him and to all these qualities. God will give you these qualities and, by doing so, give you all you need to be the best parent possible.

You raising your kids in your own power won't work. It's simply impossible. God raising your kids *through you* will work.

To Know God, You Have to Know Jesus

Becoming a Christian is all about Jesus.

There is one God, and He is the God of the Bible. There is one way to establish a relationship with God, and that is through His Son, Jesus Christ.

Here is Jesus Christ, in His own words: "I am the way, and the truth, and the life. No one comes to the Father except through me" (John 14:6).

A Christian is someone who has a personal relationship with God through Jesus. God sent Jesus to die for your sins—all the things you've done wrong—to provide forgiveness, so that you can have a relationship with God. "For God so loved the world, that he gave his only Son, that whoever believes in him should not perish but have eternal life" (John 3:16).

This is what you must believe to become a Christian: "That Christ died for our sins in accordance with the Scriptures, that he was buried, that he was raised on the third day in accordance with the Scriptures" (1 Corinthians 15:3-4).

When you believe these truths—Jesus died for your sins, He was buried, He rose from the dead—and ask Jesus to be *your* Savior, you become a Christian. You have a personal relationship with God through His Son, Jesus. You are forgiven!

You now have the power to improve your personal life. You have the power to parent. And, best of all, you're going to heaven when you die.

You Can Become a Christian—Right Now

If you are not a Christian yet, I urge you to become one. You can begin your relationship with God through Jesus right now by expressing your feelings and your decision by the words in this brief prayer:

> *Dear God, I know I am a sinner. I've made many mistakes and sinned in my life. I realize my sin separates me from You, a holy God. I believe that Your Son, Jesus Christ, died for my sins, was buried, and rose from the dead. I place my trust in Him as my Savior. I give my life to You now.*

If you prayed this prayer of belief, I am very happy for you. If you're not ready to begin a relationship with God, that's okay. What I want you to do is read the rest of this book. By the end, I think you'll see how impossible it is to raise a healthy child in your own strength. When you realize this sobering truth, I hope and pray you'll become a Christian.

Once You're a Christian, You Must Grow Spiritually

To know God through Jesus Christ is vitally important. To grow in your relationship with God is equally important. To maintain a steady supply of His power for your parenting (and all you do in life), you must stay close to Him.

A Daily Individual Quiet Time with God

To grow in your relationship with God the Father, you must spend regular time with Him. Every day invest fifteen minutes or more with God. Virtually all of your personal spiritual intimacy will occur in your daily individual times with Him.

Your quiet time with God can be at any time of the day. In a private, no-distractions-allowed quiet place, meet with God.

I want you to do three things in each quiet time.

First, begin by reading a daily devotion. This is a brief spiritual message, usually tied to a Bible passage, that helps you focus on God and spiritual things. It acts like a spiritual cup of hot chocolate: It gets your soul warmed up. There are many excellent daily devotionals, both online and hold-in-your-hands book form. Check with your pastor or Focus on the Family to find one.

Second, pray. Praying is talking with God. I say "with" because you talk to God and God speaks to you through what He has given us—the Bible. He also speaks when you sit in silence, meditate, and listen. Open up and share everything with Him: what's going on in your life, the good things He's given you, your struggles and anxieties, your fears, failures, sins, spiritual insights, spiritual doubts . . . Always take time to worship and adore Him for who He is. Never, ever, forget to thank Him for all He has done. End with your requests for Him to meet your needs and the needs of others.

Finally, read the Bible. The Bible is, quite literally, God's Word. When you read Scripture, God is talking to you: comforting, admonishing, convicting, encouraging, and teaching you. Read a short passage—a verse or several verses—and meditate on it for a few minutes. Consider how you can apply what you read to your life that very day.

While God is your most important Parenting Team member, He is not the only one. In the next chapter I'll introduce you to your other team members.

YOUR BATTLE PLAN

1. Talk about a horrible, awful, very bad, painful experience (like selling a house and buying another one) you have suffered through in the past. Who helped you survive and move ahead?

2. Do you have a personal relationship with God through His Son, Jesus? If not, what is keeping you from beginning this relationship right now?

3. If you're not ready to begin a relationship with God, will you keep an open mind about God until you finish this book?

4. If you are a Christian, how strong and close is your relationship with God? If you're struggling in this relationship, why? Are you willing to follow my quiet time actions to grow spiritually?

CHAPTER 2

YOUR HUMAN
TEAM MEMBERS

My son, Will, is a terrific golfer. Now twenty-two, he started playing at four years old. Right from the start, he was a natural. We'd play eighteen holes at our local city course, Babe Zaharias, once a week. Will would hit the ball thirty yards, run after the ball and hit it thirty more yards, run after it . . .

By age twelve, he was beating me. I'd hit my best drive off the tee and then watch him bomb his tee shot thirty yards past my ball. It takes a real man to deal with that kind of humiliation.

Will and I began to enter Best-Ball Scramble golf tournaments. In the Scramble format, there are four-man teams. On every hole, each of the four golfers hits from the same spot and you choose the best shot.

I'd ask two of my adult golfing buddies (well, they acted like adults most of the time) to join Will and me on a Scramble team. With Will hitting three-hundred-yard drives, striking crisp iron shots onto the greens, and sinking birdie putts, we usually won or finished in the top three.

Some of the other golfers in the tournaments resented being beaten by a teenager. I had zero sympathy for those losers. I'd tell them, "You could have trained your son to be a champion golfer, but you didn't. It's not my fault your son is a ballet dancer. So get used to bitter defeat."

Even though Will was far and away the best player on our Scramble teams, he couldn't win on his own. The other three players made important contributions. My two buddies and I would hit some great shots that led to low scores on holes.

God is your most important Parenting Team member. But there are four other important *human* team members. You need these four additional members to be a successful parent.

Your Church

Whether you are a Christian or not, I strongly urge you to regularly attend a local church. God wants you to be in a church (Hebrews 10:25). A good church will have a major positive impact on your life and parenting.

Your church should provide you with these benefits:

- You will grow spiritually.
- You will worship God.
- You will learn more about the Bible.
- You will serve others.
- You will make friends with other parents.
- You will get support, encouragement, and advice from the pastors, leaders, and your friends.
- Your kids will make friends with quality kids.
- Your kids will grow spiritually, worship God, learn more about the Bible, and serve others.
- Your kids will be mentored by godly, caring adult youth leaders.

When you become part of a local church, you're part of the family. And the family takes care of its own.

Your Coaches

To be an effective parent (and keep your sanity), you need at least one close friend or couple outside the home for support. For practical advice. For brainstorming with when you come up against a problem you can't figure out. For a listening ear when you have to vent about a child who's driving you nuts. For prayer.

I call these support persons—or couples—coaches because they do what coaches do: They encourage, they teach, they mentor, they motivate, and they listen. They keep you on track, strong, and focused. They help you succeed as a parent.

Look, we all have parenting problems. Don't keep yours a secret. Do what Sandy and I did. We chose some key coaches to be part of our Parenting Team. Our coaches were two couples and a single parent. We got to know these persons at our church.

When selecting your coaches, be sure these people are mature and can keep confidences. Teens can do stupid things, and having adult "friends" spread information told in confidence could damage your child's reputation.

The Bible says in Ecclesiastes 4:12: "Though a man might prevail against one who is alone, two will withstand him—a threefold cord is not quickly broken." Sandy and I have found this verse to be true. Without our coaches, our four kids would have overpowered us.

Our coaches prayed for our kids regularly. They gave much-needed support and guidance. They loved our kids and had good relationships with them. We couldn't have done a good job as parents without our coaches.

When one of our daughters was in middle school and giving us fits with her attitude and behavior, we talked the situation over with one of our coaching couples. They had a daughter who had similar issues, and they shared how they were handling it. Their support and practical ideas proved invaluable in getting our daughter back on a healthy track.

Your Family

Your family—your parents, your brothers and sisters, your uncles and aunts, your cousins—can be a key part of your Parenting Team. If your family of origin is healthy, they will love on your kids like no one else. The unconditional, loyal love of family members is a powerful force for good in the life of your children.

Sandy and I are grandparents now, and we are thrilled with this new role. Our job is to completely spoil and fawn over Izzy (six), Jackie (two), and Tyler (three months). We hug and kiss them, we play with them, we keep up with what happens in their lives, we pray for them, and we tell them everything they do is wonderful and brilliant and amazing.

Izzy lives close to us, so Chaz and Emily can dump her—I mean, leave her—with us for a few days so they can get away. They get a much needed break, and we get a much-needed three-day it's-all-about-Izzy party. Life is good.

If you have a supportive, loving family, by all means lean on them for emotional support, prayer, financial help, advice, and babysitting.

Your Babysitters

Speaking of babysitters, you need several of these team members if you hope to survive as a parent. I'm talking about babysitters who are not part of your family. Often, family members don't live near you so they can't babysit. Or, if family does live close, they may be out of town or ill or unable to babysit for some other reason.

Whether you are a single parent or a couple, you absolutely must get regular breaks from your children. If you don't, your kids really will drive you crazy. I'm not kidding. If you don't get away from them for a few hours each week, you'll be an emotional basket case: exhausted, irritable, edgy, angry, mean, impatient, intolerant, and a lot of other bad things.

If you're single, you need time to date and go out with friends. If you're married, you need time for talk, romance, and fun together. Where kids are, talk and romance and fun usually go to die.

Look for responsible, emotionally healthy teenagers or college students to babysit your kids. Talk to your church friends, neighbors, and coworkers to identify candidates. Interview each prospective babysitter.

I recommend using female babysitters. Girls are typically more mature, responsible, and nurturing than boys. Also, not many boys want to babysit.

When you interview a babysitting candidate, always do it together (if you're married) and always do it in person. Here is a list of questions to ask each candidate. I have helpfully included the acceptable answers.

1. Do you have a personal relationship with Jesus Christ?
   Answer: an immediate yes

2. How are you growing in your relationship with Jesus?
   Answer: spending time with Him regularly in prayer, devotions, and church attendance

3. What grades did you receive your last grading period?
   Answer: it better be A's and B's

4. How is your relationship with your parents?

    Answer: I love them, we get along well, I respect them

5. What kind of experience do you have caring for younger children?

    Answer: I have babysat before, I have taken care of my younger siblings, I have worked in the church nursery or children's program . . .

6. Have you ever used illegal drugs or alcohol?

    Answer: absolutely not!

Make sure you have a roster of at least three babysitters. Babysitters get sick, go out of town, have to study for big tests, and develop social lives. Try to find girls who are not dating yet. Once they start dating, it's all over. You can kiss your babysitter good-bye . . . because she's kissing Timmy.

Put babysitting money in your monthly budget. It's not cheap, but it is money well spent. Shoot for getting a babysitter once a week for at least three hours. If you can't swing once a week, make sure you have a babysitter once every two weeks.

You're thinking, "Dave, haven't you forgotten an important human Parenting Team member? I'm married, so isn't my spouse on the team?"

I haven't forgotten your spouse. If you're married, your spouse is your most important human Parenting Team member. Your marriage is so important to the success of your parenting, I'll spend the next *four* chapters talking about it.

YOUR BATTLE PLAN

1. Do you regularly attend a local church? If not, why not? Are you willing to start visiting local churches and choose one to attend?

2. Talk to persons you know who attend church and find out what churches they attend. Ask these persons questions about their churches and check out the churches' websites.

3. Can you rely on your family for help in your parenting? If not, why not? If there are family problems, are you willing to see a Christian counselor to try and fix these problems?

4. Do you have a list of at least three good babysitters? If not, why not? Do you have babysitting money in your budget? Are you willing to commit to paying a babysitter (if family can't do it) for a once-a-week, several-hour getaway?

CHAPTER 3

CLASSIC MISTAKES
MARRIED PARENTS MAKE

You'd expect me to tell you that your marriage is your most important relationship. I've spent my entire career as a psychologist—as a therapist, seminar leader, and author—working to save and improve marriages.

But don't take it from me. Take it from God. God makes it clear in the Bible that your marriage is your number one human priority. "Therefore a man shall leave his father and his mother and hold fast to his wife, and they shall become one flesh" (Genesis 2:24).

Marriage is one flesh, a complete unity of husband and wife. It is a relationship established by God Himself. Marriage is the foundation of the family.

God doesn't stop with the one-flesh truth. In Ephesians 5:25, He communicates that marriage is a sacred relationship: "Husbands, love your wives, as Christ loved the church and gave himself up for her."

Marriage—your marriage—is the very picture of Jesus Christ's relationship with the church. Wow! Just . . . wow! It doesn't get any more sacred than that.

Your Marriage Is Your Number One Priority

Nowhere in the Bible does a relationship with a child reach this level of importance and sacredness. Your children are incredibly precious to you, but they are not as precious and important as your spouse.

Nowhere in the Bible does a relationship with anyone or anything rise above your marriage.

If this is your first marriage or your fourth, it is to be—and remain—the most important human relationship in your life. Until your spouse dies, or you die.

Great Marriages Make Great Kids

All your human team members are important, but if you are married, your spouse must be at the top of the food chain. Building a great marriage will lead to two main parenting benefits.

First, you will model a healthy relationship between a husband and a wife. Your kids will have many questions about opposite sex relationships:

- How do you create and maintain intimacy?
- How do you meet real needs?
- How do you treat a woman?
- How do you treat a man?
- How do you work through conflicts?
- What role does God play in the relationship?

You know where they'll get *all* their answers? From your relationship. Your children's relationships with the opposite sex are going to be just like your relationship.

The second benefit of building a great marriage
you into an effective Parenting Team. Great parenting
teamwork. You are in a war with Satan and the cultur
in a war with your own kids!

If there is any daylight between you and your spouse, your
children will jump into it and use it to get what they want.
Divide and conquer didn't start with military generals. It started
with kids!

Avoid Ten Classic Mistakes Most Married Parents Make

Over the years of working with married couples who are parents,
I have seen these couples make the same old mistakes. These mistakes
have damaged their marriages and their kids.

Don't feel bad when you find yourself on my list of mistakes.
Chances are very good you will be guilty of a number of these mistakes. Join the club. Sandy and I made many of these mistakes as we
raised our kids.

All that matters now is to admit your mistakes and fix them to the
best of your ability. God is a God of healing and restoration. When
you fix your mistakes, you and your children will benefit.

In this chapter and the next, I'll cover ten classic mistakes. I'll
describe the mistake, the result, and the solution.

Mistake #1: Dad Not Involved

DESCRIPTION

You are not home much. You work, you spend time with your
friends, you do your own activities. Even when you are home, you're
not really home. You live in your own world. You like to do the things
you like to do, and you don't like to spend time with your kids. You
force your wife to do everything with the kids: meals, homework,
playtime, laundry, transportation . . .

RESULT

- Your wife is exhausted and resentful.
- Your wife feels abandoned by you because she *has* been abandoned by you.
- Your kids feel rejected by you because they *have* been rejected by you.
- Your kids will develop low self-esteem.

SOLUTION

- Get off your backside and get into the family.
- Make time for each child on a regular basis.
- Stop being selfish and cut back on your activities.
- Ask your wife what you can do as a dad and follow through.

Mistake #2: Mom Too Focused on the Kids

DESCRIPTION

Once you had your first child, you immediately stopped being a wife and became supermom. It's all about the kids and hardly ever about your husband. Most of your time and attention and energy go to the kids and what they need and want. Your husband gets the leftovers, and there aren't many leftovers.

RESULT

- Your husband feels rejected by you.
- Your husband is resentful and angry.
- Your marriage is dead, and you killed it.
- Your kids live in a fantasy world where they expect to get everything they want right now.

SOLUTION

- Carve out daily time with your husband.
- Give your husband the best of your attention and your energy.

- Learn to tell your kids "no" and "wait" when appropriate.
- Ask your husband what his needs are and work to meet those needs.

Mistake #3: Both Parents Too Focused on the Kids

DESCRIPTION

Both of you devote your lives to your children. Your money, your time, your attention, your energy—it all goes to the kids. Your marriage is on hold. You are just two parental units. No dates, no private conversations unless you're talking about the kids, no getaways, and no romance. No marriage, actually. Every activity is a family activity.

RESULT

- You are parents, not sweethearts and not lovers.
- You have zero intimacy.
- You're not a couple anymore, just a couple of parents.
- Once your last kid leaves your home, you will have nothing in common and nothing to talk about.
- You're teaching your kids how to have a dead, passionless marriage.

SOLUTION

- Start having private, just-the-two-of-you meetings four days a week.
- Talk about anything but the kids in these thirty-minute meetings.
- Go on a romantic date once a week (without the kids), hold hands, make out, and make love on a regular basis.
- Meet each other's needs before meeting your kids' needs.

I'm not done with my list of classic mistakes made by married parents. Brace yourself.

I cover seven more mistakes in the next chapter. Every married parent (and single parent) is on this list somewhere. Keep an open mind and have the courage to own your mistakes.

YOUR BATTLE PLAN

1. Do you believe that your marriage is sacred? Do you believe that your marriage is your most important human relationship?

2. How is your marriage doing? On a scale of one to ten (one being dead and ten being awesome), how healthy is your marriage? What are your strengths as a couple? What are your weaknesses?

3. What kind of team are you in raising your kids? What are your strengths and weaknesses as a parental team?

4. Are you guilty of any of the three classic mistakes I covered in this chapter? If so, are you willing to make changes?

5. As you continue to read the rest of my list of mistakes, are you willing to own your mistakes and work on them?

CHAPTER 4

MORE CLASSIC MISTAKES MARRIED PARENTS MAKE

IF THE THREE MISTAKES I explained in the previous chapter don't describe you as a parent, don't worry. One of the seven mistakes in this chapter will. None of us as parents are perfect. Without meaning to, we make mistakes. Mistakes that hurt our marriages and our kids.

A big part of successful parenting is identifying and correcting our mistakes. I'm helping you do that. At first, you'll hate me. But in the long run, you'll thank me for it.

Mistake #4: Stepparent Doing Discipline

DESCRIPTION

I have seen this classic mistake a million times in my work with blended families. And a million times, it has done significant damage. You, the stepparent, discipline a stepchild on your own. You decide the consequence and you deliver it to the stepchild. You do this over and over.

RESULT

- You create terrific resentment and resistance in the child.
- Every "you're not my parent" bell goes off in the child's head.
- You disrespect your spouse and his/her right to discipline their own child.

SOLUTION

- Realize it is not your job to discipline your stepchildren . . . not ever.
- Provide full input on discipline, but allow the biological parent to make the decision and deliver the consequence.

Mistake #5: One Parent in Charge

DESCRIPTION

You make all the parenting decisions. You may pretend to listen to your spouse's input, but you've already made up your mind. You know what's best, and it will be done your way.

RESULT

- You create anger, hurt, and massive frustration in your spouse.
- You cause your kids to disregard and disrespect your spouse.
- You regularly make poor parenting decisions because you don't consider your spouse's point of view.

SOLUTION

- For every parenting decision, have a full discussion with your spouse.
- With God's guidance, make the decision together.
- In a traditional marriage (first marriage with no stepkids), the father—with full input from the wife—makes the final decision.

- In a blended family (remarriage with stepchildren), the biological parent—with full input from the spouse—makes the final decision.

Mistake #6: Fighting in Front of the Kids

DESCRIPTION

You bicker and squabble in the presence of your kids. You showcase your thoughts and feelings about parenting and all kinds of personal issues.

RESULT

- You harm the self-esteem, security, and confidence of your kids.
- You damage their respect for both of you.
- Your kids will exploit your differences in an attempt to get their way.

SOLUTION

- Always deal with your conflicts—no matter what they are about—behind closed doors in private.
- If it is a parenting issue, come to a decision as a team in private and then deliver that decision to the kids.

Mistake #7: The Hero Parent

DESCRIPTION

You are the good-time, rock-and-roll, fun parent. You avoid conflict with your kids by giving them everything they want. Often, you'll agree to a parenting decision with your spouse, but later go back on it.

RESULT

- You make your spouse "the bad guy," which leads him/her to resent you (for good reason).

- You cause your spouse to be ignored and disrespected by your kids.
- You create spoiled, selfish, entitled kids.

SOLUTION

- Get a backbone and say no to the kids when needed (and it's frequently needed).
- Make parenting decisions with your spouse and stick to them.
- Realize that if a child hates you and your spouse after a decision, mission accomplished.

Mistake #8: Appeasing the Ex

DESCRIPTION

You are afraid of your former spouse and want to keep the peace. So you give in to your ex's parental plans and desires regardless of your current spouse's opinion.

RESULT

- You keep your ex happy and your spouse miserable.
- Since you are weak, you lose the respect of your spouse and your kids.
- Your kids ignore you and your spouse because they know your ex has all the parental authority.

SOLUTION

- Recognize that since you are divorced, you don't have to please your ex anymore.
- Realize that when it comes to your home and how you raise your kids in it, your ex has no say.
- Make parenting decisions only with your spouse, then communicate those decisions to your ex.

Mistake #9: Choosing Biological Kids over Your Spouse

DESCRIPTION

You have remarried, but your new spouse is not your priority—your biological kids are. You give your kids the best of your love, attention, time, and energy. When your kids disagree with your spouse, you side with your kids. When you make a decision with your spouse and your kids don't like it, you change it to make them happy.

RESULT

- You are destroying your marriage.
- As your marriage deteriorates, you will get closer and closer to your biological kids.
- You think: "If push comes to shove and I have to choose between my kids and my spouse, I'll choose my kids."

SOLUTION

- Make your marriage the most important relationship in the home.
- Choose to consider your spouse's opinions and feelings as more important than the opinions and feelings of your kids.
- Embrace the biblical truth that your relationship with your kids is not sacred, but your marriage is.

Mistake #10: Allowing Grandparents to Rule

DESCRIPTION

Your parents are meddling in your parenting and you're allowing it. Your parents give unsolicited parenting advice and you follow it. They criticize your spouse's parenting skills and you meekly say nothing to them. They drop by unannounced. They see your kids on their schedule, not yours. When they babysit, they ignore your and your spouse's guidelines and do what they want.

RESULT
- Your spouse will be furious with you and think you are a panty-waisted pushover (which you are).
- You ruin your marriage and your spouse's relationship with your parents.
- You abdicate parental authority to your parents.

SOLUTION
- Work with your spouse to develop reasonable boundaries with your parents.
- Tell your parents that you no longer want to hear unsolicited parenting advice from them; if you want their input, you'll ask for it.
- Apologize to your spouse for allowing your parents way too much control in your lives and the lives of your kids.
- Every time your parents cross a boundary, confront them with the truth.
- If your parents refuse to abide by your boundaries, let them have only limited, supervised (by you and your spouse) time with your children.

Correcting these mistakes will go a long way in protecting your marriage and keeping it strong and healthy. And in improving your effectiveness as parents.

But I want to go beyond these mistakes. To make sure your marriage is on the right track, in the next chapter I will give you my crash course on how to create and maintain an intimate marriage.

YOUR BATTLE PLAN

1. Which of the seven classic mistakes fit you? Talk about why you think you're making this mistake (or mistakes).

2. Ask your spouse (or a close friend, if you're single) which mistake or mistakes he/she sees in you. Believe this person.

3. How difficult will it be to correct your mistakes? Why will it be difficult?

4. Ask your spouse for help in fixing your mistakes. Give your spouse permission to call you out when you're making your mistakes.

CHAPTER 5

MAKE YOUR SPOUSE NUMBER ONE!

WHEN YOU MAKE the choice to have children, my friends, you give up many things.

You give up your money. Kids are incredibly expensive. You've got to feed them, clothe them, transport them, doctor them, educate them, and entertain them.

Children are, in every sense of the word, consumers. Your home is filled—right now—with expensive toys, clothes, and shoes that your kids don't even use! Am I right? Yes, I am. You'll find me right about so many things. Because I've been there!

If you have any money left when all your kids graduate from high school, now you have to pay for college. This is the final financial blow to your retirement plans. The cost of tuition is bad enough. But it is the price tag of housing and the "food plan" that will drain your bank account. *Highway robbery* is far too kind a term for what they charge for your children's dorm and cafeteria.

You and your spouse sit down with a financial adviser at the college. You dress in shabby, dirty clothes in a futile attempt to show you have no money. You ask about financial assistance. Suppressing a smirk, your adviser puts on a sad face and advises you that you make too much money to qualify for financial assistance. There will be no help for you. But you can take a mint on your way out.

You want to scream at the adviser, "I make too much money to get financial assistance, but I don't make enough money to pay for this college!" You don't bother. You've already seen several other parents dragged kicking and screaming from the financial aid office.

When you make the choice to have children, *you also give up your food.* As they grow, children eat more and more, which of course leaves you with less and less. You see, until children are twenty-one years of age, the part of their brains that tells them they're full is not fully developed. And so, they will eat until there is no food left. Like cows grazing in a pasture, your children will strip your home of food. At least, the food that tastes good. They will leave behind vegetables, prunes, and whole wheat breadsticks. Funny how that works.

The part of their brains that tells them to avoid your special snack food—candy, ice cream, that last piece of cake—is also not fully developed. You've been dreaming all day of that one special candy bar you've hidden in the freezer. You've had a hard day. You want that bar. You need that bar. It's your bar! The success or failure of your entire day rests on that one little bar. You go through your day, come home, play with the kids, and eat dinner. Then, you walk to the freezer door with confidence and anticipation. You smile as you imagine biting into your bar and tasting that smooth, creamy chocolate.

You open the door and your bar is . . . gone! You frantically rummage around, but you must face the brutal truth . . . there will be no bar for you tonight. You shut the freezer door, turn and see on the floor the empty wrapper of your bar. Well, you know what's happened. You don't even bother asking your kids. They'll just lie. Just like they've lied before. With the chocolate from your bar smeared on their faces, they'll say, "Chocolate bar? No, we didn't see a chocolate bar, Daddy."

Finally, here is the cruelest blow of all. When you have children, *you give up sex*. Remember sex? Remember how much fun it was before the children came along? I do. Oh, yes, I do. It's a cruel paradox. You must have sex to have children. But then, once you have children, you have no more sex! It's over.

You and your spouse are reduced to scheduling sex in ten- to fifteen-minute periods at odd hours, when the kids are asleep or out of your hair. Which is practically never! "Look, honey, how about next Wednesday morning from 1:00 a.m. to 1:15 a.m.? What do you think?" It's pathetic, that's what it is. The only good thing about this lack of sex is that it prevents you from having more children—which would lead to even less sex!

No one warns us that we're giving all this up. Our parents just whine for grandchildren, as though it's their right. They say nothing, because they know if we knew the truth, we'd never have kids. After we have kids, then they smirk, laugh out loud, and say, "Now you know what it's like!" These are bitter, petty people! They don't want grandchildren for pleasure. They want them for revenge!

Do Not Give Up Your Marriage!

Although I go a little overboard in my description of what you give up, it is true that you give up a lot when you have kids. Kids are a high-maintenance operation and it takes a lot of time, energy, and yes, money, to raise them the right way.

But the one thing you cannot afford to give up as parents is your marriage. It is critically important to have a strong, intimate marriage when you are raising children.

There is never a good time to have a bad marriage. But the worst time to have a bad marriage is when you have kids in the home. Your bad—or even mediocre—marriage is a huge distraction. It sucks up most of your time and energy, and it ruins your parental teamwork.

Get Your Priorities Straight

In the last two chapters, I made the case for your spouse being your number one priority. And I described ten common mistakes made by many married parents. I showed you how these ten mistakes of priority can hurt your marriage and your kids.

It's time now to identify some other things and persons that, if allowed to rise above your spouse on your list of priorities, will damage your marriage and compromise your parenting.

As I go over these nine (I tried to make it ten, but couldn't do it) misplaced priorities, be honest with yourself. What or who are you putting above your spouse on your priority list?

Your Pet

It's one thing to love your pet. It's quite another thing to love your pet more than your spouse. When you get home from work, who gets your first kiss? Who gets more of your hugs, massages, compliments, and time? Who sits on your lap when you watch television or play with your phone? Who snuggles closer to you in bed?

Your Smartphone

You are obsessed with your phone. It's your special friend, your constant companion, and your connection to the outside world. You make calls, take calls, text, and get texts. You do Facebook, Twitter, Instagram, and Snapchat. You play games, watch tons of short videos, check the news, and get weather reports.

When you drop your phone, you panic. When your phone goes dead, you panic. When you lose your phone, you panic. Without your phone, you are helpless. Paralyzed. You'd call 911, but you can't because you don't have your phone!

When you're with your spouse at home, you're on your phone. When the two of you are in the car, you're on your phone. When you're in bed together—I'm serious here—you're on your phone. When the two of you are in a restaurant, you're on your phone.

Your Work

Hello, my name is Dave, and I'm a workaholic. If you're like me, you spend too many hours at work. Even when you're home, you're doing work or thinking about work. You're driven, and you are also driving your spouse away.

Your Hobby

Whatever you enjoy doing in your spare time, you do to excess. You play a sport. You fish. You hunt. You watch sports on television. You are in several fantasy leagues. You work on old cars. You bowl. You do crafts. You sew. You scrapbook. You shop. You play golf.

Your TV

You love watching your favorite shows on your television, your phone, or your computer. You have cable. You have Netflix. You have whatever service you need to access your shows. You have too many favorite shows, and you spend too many hours watching them. You think the characters on those shows are real and they are your friends.

Your Exercise

Keeping your body toned, fit, sculpted, and in shape is your top priority. Along with your overkill workout schedule, you eat a precisely balanced, unbelievably nutritious diet. No sugar. No gluten. No salt. No preservatives. No taste. Unless you're training for the Olympics, you're going too far.

Your Friends

Even though you're married, your friends take up a lot of your time and attention. It hasn't dawned on you that you're married now and you need to spend more time with your spouse than your friends. As my daughter Emily told her new husband, Chaz, a year into their marriage: "You are being single Chaz. I need you to be married Chaz."

Your Church

You are overcommitted at your church. You are on everyone's short list for volunteers because you never say no. Church jobs are usually like the Supreme Court: They are lifetime appointments. You're serving God, which is good. But you are neglecting your spouse, which is bad.

Your House

You are continually working on your house. You do chores, you clean, and you putter. You fix things, you redecorate, and you move furniture around. You also spend hours and hours on your lawn and landscaping. Your home looks fabulous! Too bad your marriage is dying.

Ask Your Spouse Three Questions

Have *the conversation*. Do it today, not tomorrow. Because you won't do it tomorrow. In a private place, with just the two of you, ask your spouse three questions:

1. "In my life, what is above you on my priority list?" Whatever your spouse says, don't be defensive. Don't deny. Don't disagree. Don't justify. Believe what your spouse says. Own it! The correct response is: "You're right. I'm sorry. I'm going to change."

2. "How can I put my substitute priority in its place?" Then do what your spouse wants you to do to eliminate or cut back on your substitute priority.

3. "How can I make you my number one priority?" Your spouse will tell you what you can do, and your job is to do it.

- more time together
- deeper conversations
- more physical intimacy
- going out on dates
- more household chores
- more romance
- praying together

Ask for specific, detailed actions and do them.

Which Conversation Do You Want to Have?

The above conversation is a difficult one. But it's a whole lot easier than this conversation: "I don't love you anymore, and I want a divorce."

I'm telling you, you'd better have the first conversation about your priority in life. Because if you don't have that conversation, you'll have the second conversation.

Once you've decided to make your spouse your top priority, you need to work on building real intimacy in three areas: emotional, spiritual, and physical.

I'm going to help you do that right now.

YOUR BATTLE PLAN

1. Talk about how much money, food, sex, and other things you've given up for your kids.

2. How has your marriage suffered since you had kids? Why is it suffering?

3. Which of these nine priorities is above your spouse? Why is your priority person or activity above your spouse? Why is this person or activity so important to you?

4. Have the conversation today, ask the three questions, and start putting your spouse first.

CHAPTER 6

HOW TO BE
HAPPILY MARRIED . . .
WITH KIDS

I'VE GOT TWO WORDS for you married parents who want to build an intimate relationship: boarding school.

I'm kidding. It's tempting on some days, but these schools are way too expensive. And you love your kids and want them to live with you.

When I was in high school English literature classes, I was forced to read the "classics." To be considered a classic, a book has to be incredibly long, incredibly boring, and incredibly hard to read. The only persons who read these classics voluntarily are high school English literature teachers.

Faced with the prospect of having to read these weighty tomes, I turned to the special friend of high school English literature students everywhere: CliffsNotes. Mr. Cliffs, or whoever invented these Notes, is a genius. He, or she, should receive the Nobel Peace Prize and the Pulitzer, and be added to Mount Rushmore.

Why? Because CliffsNotes offered a brief, accurate outline of these classic books. I didn't have to read these books! Not even a word! All I had to do was peruse the CliffsNotes summary and I was good to go.

CliffsNotes for Marriage

In this chapter I'm going to give you the CliffsNotes on how to build an intimate marriage when you have kids in your home. I'll cover the three essential areas of marital intimacy: emotional, spiritual, and physical.

Emotional Intimacy

Definition: Each week, developing deeper conversations and meeting each other's real needs.

Couple Talk Times

On Saturday or Sunday, the husband sits down with his wife and schedules four thirty-minute Couple Talk Times for the upcoming week. These talks will be held in a warm, cozy, private place in your home. It will be just the two of you, with no distractions allowed. No kids. No pets. No television. No electronic devices.

The Wife Shares in Two Categories

The first category, which comprises 85 percent of what she shares, is what I call "I'm going to bring up a number of topics and you can decide which ones to respond to." She shares with no expectation of a response by her husband. If he's interested in one of the topics, he'll give a response and they'll have a dialogue.

Fifteen percent of what she shares falls into the second category: "I need a response to this topic." Once the husband knows she needs a response, he will process what she shares and give his personal response. They'll have a dialogue on this topic.

The Husband Needs Time to Process

The wife must give her husband time and space to process the information and emotions she shares. A man is unable to give an immediate, deeper response. Often, he will give his response at the next scheduled Couple Talk Time.

Carryover Topics

You only develop a deeper conversation when the two of you talk about a topic multiple times. Using your four Couple Talk Times, you have four conversations about one topic over the course of a week. Each time you discuss a topic in a Talk Time, you get a little deeper.

Ask for Your Spouse's Needs Twice a Day

If you don't know what your spouse's needs are, you can't meet them. The only way to find out what these needs are is to ask. In the morning, before you leave, ask: "What are your needs today? What can I do for you?" In the evening, right when you get home, ask again: "What can I do for you tonight?"

Spiritual Intimacy

Definition: Each week, putting God at the center of your relationship by praying together, having spiritual conversations, and reading the Bible together.

Pray Together Four Times a Week

Pray for five minutes during each of your four Couple Talk Times. Make a list of requests, choose which items you will each pray for, and pray one at a time. Pray out loud, and hold hands.

Have Spiritual Conversations Two Times a Week

Talk about your individual spiritual lives during at least two of your four Couple Talk Times. Tell your spouse, in detail, what is happening in your relationship with God:

- what you're doing in your daily quiet time with God
- insights you've gained in your Bible reading
- how you're applying the Bible to your life
- spiritual victories and defeats
- how God is guiding you every day

Read the Bible Together Once a Month

Choose one week a month to read and study a Bible passage together. During your first Couple Talk Time of that week, read out loud a passage of Scripture—one verse or several verses. Briefly discuss the verses and give your initial reactions. Once a day for the next four or five days, you each read the passage and meditate on it. At the end of the week, during your final Couple Talk Time, you each share the results of your meditation.

Physical Intimacy

Definition: Each week, enjoying physical touch by kissing, making out, giving massages, and having intercourse.

Kiss, Make Out, and Give Massages

As wonderful and important as intercourse is in a married couple's life, it is not enough to satisfy your need for physical intimacy. Non-intercourse touching through daily kissing, making out, and giving massages will keep you connected and prepare you for your times of sexual intercourse.

Also important are romantic words and actions, playful behaviors, and flirting. These daily expressions of love, coupled with non-intercourse touching, will boost your sexual bond and energize your physical desire.

Have Regular Intercourse

If you don't schedule your times of intercourse, you won't have them. Or at least not as often as needed. So schedule them. Scheduling intercourse also helps you prepare and heightens your anticipation of this wonderful event.

Every couple disagrees on how often intercourse should take place. That's normal. Have honest conversations about frequency and reach compromises. You should be making love on a regular basis, but you have to decide how often regular is.

How Is Your Marriage Doing?

This is obviously a very brief, incomplete overview of what it takes to build an intimate marriage. For an in-depth look at emotional and spiritual intimacy, get my book *Men Are Clams, Women Are Crowbars*. For practical ideas on how to create romance and a sizzling sex life, get my book *Kiss Me Like You Mean It*.

You can't afford to have a weak, unhappy marriage when you're raising kids. The quality of your parenting is directly related to the quality of your marriage.

If your marriage is going well and you are happy and close, this chapter will serve as a refresher course to keep you on track and give you ways to improve.

If your marriage is struggling, this chapter will make it painfully apparent that you need help. Locate a licensed Christian counselor in your area and schedule an appointment. Right now.

To find a solid, effective therapist, ask your pastor or contact Focus on the Family at FocusontheFamily.com or 1-800-afamily.

Now I will turn my attention to single parents. There are some important things I want you unmarried parents to know before we dive into my parenting Battle Plan.

YOUR BATTLE PLAN

1. How are you doing in the area of emotional intimacy? Are you making time to talk in a private place four times a week? If not, are you willing to do this?

2. How many deep conversations do you have each week? Do my ideas on deeper communication (the wife sharing in two categories, the husband taking time to process, and carryover topics) make sense to you? Are you willing to try these communication strategies? What would stop you from trying these?

3. Ask your spouse how you're doing meeting his/her needs. Ask your spouse what his/her top three needs are.

4. Are you willing to ask about your spouse's needs twice a day?

5. What is your level of spiritual intimacy as a couple? How often do you pray together? How often do you have spiritual conversations? How often do you read the Bible together?

6. Are you willing to start doing these three spiritual intimacy behaviors? What would stop you from doing them?

7. Talk honestly about your physical intimacy. What's happening in the kissing, making out, and giving massages departments?

8. Are you both happy and satisfied with your lovemaking? Is intercourse happening often enough? When you do have intercourse, what is the experience like for each of you? How can you improve?

9. If your marriage is weak in one or more of these three areas of intimacy, are you willing to take action to improve? Will you get one of my marriage books, read it together, and apply my action steps?

10. If your marriage is struggling and you are unhappy, are you willing to see a Christian therapist immediately?

CHAPTER 7

SINGLE PARENTING: TOUGHER THAN ELEPHANT TRAINING

EVERY YEAR all the major media outlets release a list of the most difficult, dangerous, and stressful jobs in America. These usually make the top five:

Dynamite factory worker
SWAT team member
Firefighter
Special Forces operative
Elephant trainer

These jobs certainly should make the list. But these annual lists always omit the toughest job of all: single parent. And I'm not kidding.

Single parenting is a never-ending, relentless, exhausting treadmill. No breaks. No downtime. No sleeping in. No opportunity to have a coherent series of rational thoughts. Your kids have a lot of needs, and guess who has to meet them?

Their problems. Their crises. Their tantrums. Their homework. Their laundry. Their meals. Their birthday parties and the birthday parties of their friends. Their questions. Their acting out. Their fears. Their moods. Their . . .

You do it all for your kids. Every time. You have to. It's just you on the job. You are raising your kids, running a home, and making a living.

You're doing all this while at the same time trying to maintain some kind of personal life. Okay, go ahead and laugh now. How in the world can you have a personal life?

Oh, and you also have to deal with whatever issues your ex brings to the table. That's another story.

Of course, you love your kids dearly, and you have plenty of great times with them. But it's still a brutal grind. There are times when you want to just scream your head off. There are times when you just want to quit. There are times when you wonder if you can make it another day.

In this chapter I want to cover some foundational self-care principles for you single parents.

Take Care of Yourself

I know you know this truth, but I'm going to state it anyway: You must take care of yourself because no one else will. Your kids won't because they're kids and they think of themselves. Your ex won't; that's why he/she is an ex.

No one on your support team, including God, will meet your needs unless *you* do your part. No one will come through for you unless *you* build the relationships and ask for help.

Many single parents have said to me: "Dave, I'm the kind of person who hates to ask for help. I don't want to bother people. I'll just rely on myself." My response is always the same: "Get over it. If you don't get regular, significant help, you will burn out. You will hurt yourself and your kids. You will fail as a parent. You need help!"

Build a Robust Support Team and Lean on It!

You've read the chapters on your Parenting Team members. Every parent, married or single, needs a team. As a single parent, you don't just need a support team. You need a *world-class* team. You need a team on steroids.

Let me show you the kind of Parenting Team you need to build.

God

Every parent needs a close, strong relationship with God. As a single parent, yours has to be closer and stronger. Make sure you have a daily quiet time with God. In this quiet time, read a devotion, and read, pray, and meditate on a Bible passage. Spend at least twenty minutes with God.

As you go through your day, be aware of God's presence and continue to talk to Him and seek His strength and guidance. When you are stressed by life, work, others, and your kids, call out for God's help.

Church

Make your church your second home. Don't just attend the worship services. Get involved and get your kids involved. Get into a small group that meets on Sunday morning or during the week. These small-group members will be part of your Parenting Team.

Get your kids into the children's programs and youth programs. Your kids will grow spiritually and make quality friends. Get to know the parents of your kids' friends. These parents may transport your kids places and have them over to their homes. Plus, these parents can be excellent role models for your kids. It's also important to have your kids' friends over to your house often so you get to know them—and know what your kids and their friends are doing.

Coaches

You'll be shocked to read this, but you need more than one close friend or couple to be on your coaching team. You have more needs, so you need more coaches. Cultivate at least two close friends for coaches. Three is even better. These coaches will not only support and mentor you, but they will also support and mentor your children.

Your coaches will babysit for you. They will transport your kids at times. They will listen to you vent, cry, and complain about your kids and your stressful life. They will talk you through periods of crisis and give you practical parenting strategies. They will pray with you. They will build a good relationship with each of your kids and provide them with love and guidance.

Family

Unless your family members are crazy or abusive, do not hesitate to ask for their assistance. Whatever they can do for you, you want them to do. If they are local, sign them up for a wide variety of your parenting needs. If they're out of town, they can still support you with a listening ear, money, gifts, and prayer.

Babysitters

Three babysitters won't cut it. Get four or five for your list. When you need a break from your wonderful children, you absolutely and positively have to have it. Babysitters enable you to create a personal life, build friendships, go to your small group, shop, date, goof off, and get recharged.

Your Ex

If your relationship with your ex is at all cordial, he or she has a role to play as part of the Parenting Team. Those are his/her children too, so think of ways to work together for the good of your kids. Naturally, this is not always possible.

Build a big, strong parenting team. Ask for help, and don't stop asking. Tell each member to be honest with you and say no if needed. If you get a no from anyone—except God—move on to another team member.

I have laid a solid foundation for your parenting journey. Whether you are married or single, in a traditional or blended marriage, you and your team are ready to go to work.

Now it's time to go over my comprehensive, detailed battlefield briefing.

YOUR BATTLE PLAN

1. What's the toughest job you've ever had? How does that job compare to the job of being a single parent?

2. How well do you take care of yourself? Currently, what needs are not being met in your life?

3. Do you have trouble asking others for help? If so, why is this so hard?

4. Who is on your Parenting Team now? Who could you add?

5. Of the Parenting Team members I mentioned, which one will be the hardest to sign up? Why?

PART TWO

Needs

CHAPTER 8

IT'S ALL ABOUT THE RELATIONSHIP

As a full-time therapist for the past thirty years, I'm in the relationship-building business. When I see a client, male or female, in individual therapy, I do a number of things. I take a thorough history, make a diagnosis, identify all aspects of the problem, and devise a plan of action.

All these steps are helpful, but they are meaningless unless I establish a good relationship with my client. All change, all growth, and all improvement come through relationship.

If I am unable to click with a client and build a good relationship, the therapy won't work. It can't work. My client won't open up, won't do homework, and will stop coming to see me.

For therapy to be successful, my clients have to know and believe these things about me:

- I care about them.
- I can be trusted.
- I want the best for them.
- I will do my best for them.
- I will always tell them the truth.
- I will never give up on them.

Parenting Is a Lot Like Therapy

Just as in therapy, it is essential for you to build a good relationship with each of your children. A healthy, loving relationship is the *core principle* of my parenting Battle Plan. The relationship is what makes it work.

A solid relationship with a child bonds the two of you together. It communicates caring and love. It ensures that your child will trust you, listen to you, and follow your guidance. It keeps you connected, even during difficult times when your child hates you and is rejecting you.

Sandy and I worked hard to build a close relationship with each of our four children. We believe these relationships were the key to our successful parenting. We were not perfect parents, and we did not raise perfect kids. But we did a good job. A nice benefit is that now we are great friends with our adult children!

How to Build a Good Relationship with a Child

Every child has five critical needs. When you meet these needs in your child's life, you get two wonderful outcomes. First, your child becomes a successful, godly person. Second, you build a strong, intimate relationship with your child.

In this section of the book, I show you exactly how to meet these five core needs. Here's a brief preview.

①Love

The most basic human need. It bonds you and your child forever. It leads to a healthy love of self. It is critical for self-esteem and security.

②Respect

Respect is just behind love in importance. It involves respect for self and others. It establishes healthy boundaries in relationships. It creates trust. It's vital to building healthy relationships with others.

③Competence

Confidence and direction come from competence. Finding your strengths is good for career and for hobbies and interests. Competence develops identity.

④Spirituality

By helping your child begin a relationship with God and grow in that relationship, you meet the most important need of all. Spirituality provides purpose in life and the power to live that life in a way that pleases God.

⑤Independence

The ability to live on your own is a central part of being an adult. You launch your children so they can make meaningful contributions to society and to God's Kingdom.

The Parenting Three-Step

First Step: You meet these five needs so your child is a successful, godly person.

Second Step: By meeting these five needs, you build a strong relationship with your child.

Third Step: It is the relationship that makes your parenting—your teaching, guidance, modeling, and discipline—effective.

So, How Is Your Relationship with Each Child?

To get a baseline reading of the quality of your relationship with each of your children, I want you to do an evaluation. In that evaluation, you will ask these three questions:

- What am I doing right in my relationship with each child?
- What am I doing to weaken my relationship with each child?
- What can I do to make the relationship better?

Ask these three questions of each of these persons:

- yourself
- your spouse (if married)
- your romantic partner (if not married)
- your best friend
- your parents
- each of your children

If you've got the guts to ask these questions of these individuals, you'll get a good picture of your relationship with each child.

Now let me show you how to meet these five essential needs and, at the same time, build a close, vibrant relationship with each of your precious children.

YOUR BATTLE PLAN

1. What kind of relationship did your dad build with you? What could he have done better? Answer these two questions about your relationship with your mom.

2. What is your answer to the three questions about your relationship with each child?

3. Share your self-evaluation with your spouse or boyfriend/ girlfriend and then ask this person to answer the three questions about you.

4. Ask the three questions of your best friend, your parents, and each child.

5. Based on what you find out from yourself and these persons close to you, how can you improve your relationship with each of your children?

CHAPTER 9

"PLEASE LOVE ME"

Pacifier. It sounds so sweet. So soothing. So gentle. Such a helper and friend to a parent. Just pop a pacifier in, and your child is happy, content, and . . . well . . . pacified. Yeah. Right. As a brand-new parent, I believed these shameless lies cranked out by the pacifier industry. I found out the hard way that the pacifier was no friend of mine. It made my life a living nightmare for two solid years. Since *60 Minutes* doesn't have the guts to expose the pacifier hoax, I'll do it myself.

Our first child (and very nearly our last), Emily, became extremely attached to the first pacifier we put into her mouth. It was like she bonded to that pacifier and not to us. We, her own caring parents, couldn't comfort her when she was upset. We couldn't quiet her down. The only thing that worked was the pacifier. She had to have that pacifier to stop crying. She had to have that pacifier to take a nap. She had to have that pacifier to get to sleep at night. Every night, when it was bedtime, Emily would say, "Brush the teeth, and pacifier." It became a ritual set in stone.

She knew that pacifier intimately: every curve, every stain, every tooth mark. It was the only pacifier she'd take into her screaming, whining, pouting little mouth.

We bought three others just like it, but she refused to accept them. She'd immediately spit the imposter out of her mouth, throw it on the floor, and yell, "That's not my pacifier!" You know what happened next, don't you? We'd have to turn the house upside down looking for that no-good, stupid, time-wasting, blood-sucking, $1.99 pacifier! Oh, I can remember as though it were yesterday those mad, desperate searches. Emily would throw that pacifier down in the strangest places, and, of course, she'd never know where it was. That wasn't *her* problem.

Sandy and I were slaves to that pacifier. It ran our miserable lives.

I hated that pacifier, but I was powerless against it. But then one beautiful day, the sun broke through and light shone into my dark world of torment. It was the day we broke Emily's pacifier habit. I will never forget that day. She called for her pacifier at bedtime, but she didn't get it. She screamed and yelled and sobbed for one solid hour. Sandy was upset and felt sorry for Emily. I pretended to be sympathetic, but I was a happy man. I was finally being released from prison.

The next day, I took the pacifier outside and placed it on the cold, hard concrete driveway. I said to it, "It's over, Pacifier! You've had a nice run, but it's over. Now you pay for your crimes." I took my trusty hammer and crushed the pacifier into little pieces. Then I threw my head back and, in a loud voice, said, "Free at last! Free at last! I'm finally free at last!"

Why do small kids get so attached to pacifiers, blankets, stuffed animals, and other objects? It's because kids are sensitive, tenderhearted little creatures. It's not easy being small in a big world. Kids have insecurities and fears. Those special objects help children cope with the scary parts of life. They offer a certain measure of comfort and security. "It's not just me in this big, dark room. It's me and my pacifier." Or "Me and my teddy bear." So it's perfectly okay to give your kids these objects. Go ahead and search for them when they get lost.

But parents, you need to realize that these objects provide only a temporary and superficial solution to your children's fears of being alone and vulnerable. Over the long term, real security and comfort come only when you meet the deepest need of your children. That need is love.

Love Is Everything

I define love this way: to feel you belong, that you are unconditionally accepted by at least one person on the face of the earth.

The apostle Paul's great chapter on love, 1 Corinthians 13, makes it clear how important love is. The final verse in this chapter, verse 13, says it all: "So now faith, hope, and love abide, these three; but the greatest of these is love."

Without love, we have nothing. Without love, we are nothing. Love is the greatest human need.

Your child has a desperate need to be loved by you. Your job as a parent is to make your love for your child crystal clear. This will give her a foundation to stand on when everything else in her world is chaotic. Growing up is tough and getting tougher all the time. Knowing she is loved, and feeling that love, gives her the confidence to face the world and win.

Love is action. Doing loving things is what communicates love. Parents tell me all the time, "I love my kids. I really do. I'm sure they know it." My response is, "How? How do they know it?" You'd better make good and sure they know it. Love not communicated is worthless. It's nothing. It's not love at all. Here are some actions that any parent, single or married, can do to communicate love to a child.

The Every-Days

As our four kids grew up, Sandy and I did three things every day to communicate love to our children. This system worked for us and it will work for you.

Say "I Love You"

First, say "I love you" to each child. These are the most beautiful words in any language. They are healing words. Use the child's name to make it personal. "I love you, Emily." "I love you, Leeann." "I love you, Nancy." "I love you, Will." Do this at least once a day.

I can't tell you how many times I've heard these words in my therapy office from adult clients: "Dave, my dad—or mom—never said to me, 'I love you.'" These clients are usually sobbing when they tell me this. They want desperately to hear those words, but many never will. I've heard many stories of clients waiting in vain by the deathbed of a parent, hoping to hear, "I love you." It's heartbreaking. It's not right! If you can't say these words, take speech lessons. Get therapy.

Some of you are thinking, "But Dave, I didn't hear 'I love you' growing up. I'm not an expressive person. I show love in other ways." My response is: "Get over it!" If you don't say these words once a day, damage is done.

Give a Physical Touch

The second daily action is physical touch. Touch every one of your kids in an affectionate, caring way every day. A hug. A kiss. A rub on the neck. A squeeze on the shoulder.

What's the largest organ in the human body? It's the skin! God could have covered us with sandpaper or fishhooks, but He didn't do that. He covered us with skin because it's supposed to be touched.

Touch feels warm. It feels caring. It feels like love.

It's easier to touch with young children. Most of the time they run to you and begin touching. Older children are tougher to touch. All of a sudden, your teens have personal space requirements.

When our kids were small, I'd come home from work and hit the garage door opener. Before the garage door was halfway up, all four of my kids would run to the car and smother me with hugs and kisses. "Daddy's home! We love you, Daddy! Mommy's mean, so mean."

Once our kids hit middle school, it was a very different scene when I got home and hit the garage door opener. No one came out. Sandy would eventually come out and say: "The kids aren't coming out, Daddy. They hate you now too."

If you have a teenager, you've got to be clever. Take off your shoes and sneak up behind your teen and squeeze his shoulder. He'll flinch and say, "Oh, man, cut it out!" But deep down, he'll like it. Teens need touch as much as, if not more than, younger kids.

Some of you are thinking, "But, Dave, I'm just not an affectionate person. Touch is just not my thing." My response is: "Get over it!" It'll be awkward at first, but you'll get the hang of it.

Share One Personal Item

The third Every-Day action is to share one personal item. By personal, I mean a feeling, a need, a painful experience, a victory, or a spiritual insight. When you share something personal, it means "I love you."

This means opening up and showing your kids a piece of who you are inside. This kind of vulnerability creates a love connection between parents and children. Also, it models sharing. When you share, it's more likely the kids will open up and share. It sends the message: "In this family, we openly share our feelings, and talk honestly and personally."

Some of you are thinking, "But Dave, I've never been an expressive person. I'm very private and don't share personal things." Guess what my response is. "Get over it." If you don't share personally on a regular basis, your kids won't know you and they won't feel loved by you.

A good time to share your one personal item is bedtime. Your kid's in bed and you spend a few minutes with her. It's quiet and relaxed at the end of the day. If your kid is strong-willed, difficult, or in middle school, most of the mean is gone.

Actually, you can use these few minutes at bedtime to do all three Every-Days. You can say "I love you," do a physical touch, and share one personal item.

Some of you don't see your child every day. Don't worry. On the days you can't be with your child physically, you can still say "I love you" and share one personal item. That's what smartphones and other electronic devices are for. When you do see your child in person, you can do the physical touch action.

You Gotta Spend Time

For children of all ages, love is measured in time. Without time, there is no love. There couldn't be. Without time together, there is no personal relationship. When the right amount of time is provided, love is clearly and powerfully communicated. You ask, "How much time and what kind of time?"

One-on-one time is the best way to communicate love and build the relationship. I recommend you offer several hours of individual time to each child once every two or three weeks. I say "offer" because teenagers won't always take you up on invitations. After a certain age, being seen with Mom or Dad is the absolute kiss of social death.

You suddenly become a leper—someone to be tolerated, pitied, and avoided at all costs. Teens will take your money, but your presence is not welcomed. However, if you're willing to do an activity your teen really enjoys, you just might entice the kid to spend time with you.

In this individual time, do what the kid wants to do. Forcing a kid to tag along on your activity of choice does not communicate love. It communicates selfishness. It doesn't matter if you don't like your kid's chosen activity. It's even better if you don't like it, because then your kid really knows you love him. For years my dad played golf with me because I loved the game. My dad hated golf, and he wasn't very good at it. As I watched my dad struggle around the golf course, hitting one horrendous shot after another, I knew two things were true: First, my dad was a terrible golfer. Second, my dad loved me.

I'm talking about one-on-one time between fathers and sons, mothers and daughters, fathers and daughters, and mothers and sons. Don't fall into the common trap of just investing time with your same-sex kids. No, no, no! It's easier and more natural for moms to focus on daughters and dads to focus on sons. But this robs your opposite-sex kids of the chance to get to know you and feel loved by you.

When my three girls got older and finally left the Barbie stage—thank God—I took them on lunch dates. I played Barbies with my little sweeties for years, but I was ready to move on.

My girls wanted to go out to lunch, so that's what we did. It gave them the opportunity to do what they enjoyed most: talk.

My preteen girls wanted it to be a real date, so here's what I had to do. With my date watching from the window, I'd go outside and get in my car. I'd get out of my car and walk to my front door and ring the doorbell.

My date would say in a sweet voice, "Who is it?" I'd think to myself, "What do you mean, who is it? You just saw me walking up to the door." Of course, I didn't say that. I'd say, "It's Daddy, your date."

I'd go to the restaurant my date selected. I'd hold the car door open for her. I'd hold her hand as we walked. I'd get her chair at the restaurant. I'd listen to her talk . . . and talk, and talk, and talk. And I'd have a wonderful time. And so would she.

I played sports with my son, Will. He has always been a sports fanatic: baseball, football, basketball, you name it. But his favorite sport (and mine, coincidentally) is golf. I started taking him to a local golf course when he was four years old.

We played golf together for years. And while we played golf, we talked about girls and school and God and life.

Critical need number two is respect. Let's take a good look at that need next.

YOUR BATTLE PLAN

1. Share a pacifier story. How did you eventually wean your kids off the pacifier?

2. How did your parents do in loving you? Did they do the Every-Days? How could your parents have been better in meeting your need for love?

3. Of my three Every-Days ("I love you," a Physical Touch, and Share One Personal Item), which will be the hardest for you to do? Why?

4. How much one-on-one time do you spend with each of your children in a two-week period? Do you do what you want to do or what they want to do?

CHAPTER 10

"PLEASE RESPECT ME"

THE FOURTEEN-YEAR-OLD person came in the door of my office, just ahead of her parents. I say "person" because at first glance, I couldn't tell what sex I had on my hands. The parents shuffled in, looking like refugees from a lost war. They looked uneasy, as though they were both about to throw up. I was soon to understand the reason for their chronic feeling of nausea.

As the family of three settled into their chairs, I took a good, long look at the girl. What a sight! She had spiked hair with orange and blue clumps shooting up at random angles. Pieces of string and jewelry were tied around some of the hair clumps. She wore makeup that would have made a supermodel jealous. It was bright white and at least a foot thick. Her earrings were as big as wind chimes. Of course, she didn't just have earrings on her ears. It looked as if every available spot on her body had been pierced and a ring inserted—a ring through her eyebrow, a ring through her nose, a ring through her tongue, and a ring through her navel. She was apparently proud of her navel ornament because it was on display. She wore wild, striped clothes that looked like they'd been salvaged from the site of a seventies disco museum. The girl looked like an alien, pure and simple. As a shrewd and tactful therapist, I knew it was important to gain the girl's trust and build rapport as quickly as possible. So I said to her, "Where's your spaceship, sweetheart?" I thought her parents were going to have a conniption right there in my office. The kid actually got a kick out of my question. After my rather ragged beginning, I took a history and found out what I already knew: This girl had no respect. No respect for herself. No respect for her parents. No respect for anyone. Not even her weird friends.

Her parents were permissive, and they were paying a dear price for their parenting style. This girl had zero self-esteem, because without respect, self-esteem dies. Her outrageous appearance and contempt for her parents masked a deep sense of personal shame and self-loathing. The main presenting problem was that she had decided to stop attending school. She was, in fact, refusing to do anything her parents wanted her to do.

The key to the case was building respect. As the parents got tough and laid down clear limits and consequences, the girl began to respect them. As communication improved in the family, she began to earn her parents' respect. Finally, she began to respect herself. Her clothing even improved. She wasn't wearing dresses, but at least she didn't look like a character from *Star Wars*.

The Nightmare of No Respect

This is just one example of what can happen when a child has no respect. Believe me, it can get a lot worse. If you don't meet the need of respect, you'll create a teenager—and then an adult—with a list of nasty traits:

- arrogance
- self-centeredness
- entitlement
- no respect for authority
- no concern for the needs of others
- no ability to work with others or build healthy relationships
- no tolerance for pain or disappointment

To avoid this awful scenario, let's look at some practical ways to meet the need for respect in your child's life.

Definition

I define respect this way: establishing clear boundaries between you and others. A person with respect knows the limits between himself and others. He doesn't cross the line to mistreat others, and doesn't allow others to mistreat him without responding.

Respect is essential to building good, stable, close relationships with others. If a child has respect, he will treat himself and others with dignity, concern, and fairness. He will not destroy himself or let others destroy him.

Know Your Limits

You build respect into your children with limits—and there are two kinds of limits. First, there are the limits you place on your children. You set clear boundaries in your home and enforce them consistently. You draw up—with your spouse and support system—the rules of the house. You present these rules to your children and say, "Here are the boundaries of your life. We believe staying inside these boundaries is what the Lord wants. They will keep you safe and help you develop into healthy and godly persons. If you decide to cross a boundary, we will apply consequences." I go into detail on these kinds of limits in my chapters on discipline.

Limits of the second type are those you allow your children to place on you. Many parents aren't aware that limits go both ways. Respect your child's privacy. Knock before entering your child's room. This is common courtesy. I had to learn this with my three daughters. I didn't want to barge in when they were dressing and embarrass them and myself. They had to knock on my door, so it's only right that I knocked on their doors. Don't misunderstand me, I'm the parent and I owned the house. So I was going to come into the room. They were not allowed to keep me out. But I could grant them the respect of waiting a few minutes. "Are you ready to receive your honored visitor, my dear?"

Unless you have solid justification, don't read your kid's mail, texts, emails, Facebook posts, tweets, or diaries. Don't listen in on her phone conversations. Don't go through her phone. Don't search or tidy up her room. It's better for your health to stay out of her room, anyway.

If you have a good reason, however, don't hesitate to violate every area of your child's privacy. If you suspect trouble, go through the kid's room with a fine-tooth comb. Go through her phone and read everything in there. Check out all her digital activity. Talk to her friends, other parents, and school officials.

Here are some common good-enough reasons to violate a child's privacy: social withdrawal, dropping grades, acting out at school and at home, a very sad and unhappy mood that lasts more than a month, dropping out of activities she usually enjoys, blatant disrespect and verbal abuse of you, avoiding old friends and hanging out with questionable companions, extreme fatigue, bursts of intense anger . . .

Your kid will scream bloody murder and threaten never to forgive you. Fine. Forgiveness isn't the issue. Correcting a serious problem and saving your child is the issue.

Your child will throw this classic line at you: "You don't trust me." You respond immediately and calmly, "Based on your behavior, no, I don't. You'll have to earn back my trust." As President Ronald Reagan used to say about the Russian leaders, "Trust but verify."

Communicate to Build Respect

You also meet the need for respect in your children with communication skills. Communicating effectively with children is incredibly difficult. They're immature, and they don't yet have the tools to communicate well. It's your job as the parent to teach them the basic skills of connecting in a conversation. When you teach these skills, you'll build more than just a good relationship. You'll build respect.

You need to learn to listen to your child. James 1:19 gives us a great communication principle: "Know this, my beloved brothers: let every person be quick to hear, slow to speak, slow to anger." Many parents (including me) are slow to listen, quick to speak, and quick to get angry with their children. I worked hard on listening, and I want you to work at it too.

So many conversations with a kid are lost in the first few sentences because the parent reacts, cuts in, and interrupts. My fellow parents, if you want your kid to listen to you, you've got to model by listening to him. If you want to keep a conversation alive, you've got to listen. The first thing—the very first thing—you do when your child speaks, is listen. Say nothing. Just listen with your big mouth closed.

After your child has gotten several paragraphs out and is warming up, you can move to the second thing. Reflect your child's emotions. Notice that you still have not said anything original in this conversation. And you won't for a while.

By reflecting, you can communicate understanding of your child's emotions, whatever they are—anger, hurt, humiliation, frustration, fear, joy . . . Your child feels understood when you identify and give back her emotions. In other words, it's all about what your kid is saying and feeling in the first part of a conversation. "Is this what you are feeling about what you are saying, Susan?"

You will have all kinds of thoughts and feelings as your kid talks. Stuff these until it's your turn. If you jump in before you communicate understanding, you violate respect, and the conversation is over. You may be talking, but no one's going to be listening. Why should your kid listen to you? You weren't listening to her.

As in the case of limits, there is an exception to this. You don't bother reflecting when your kid is out of control: yelling, using profanity, or being verbally abusive. When Jimmy has lost it and is tearing into you verbally, you don't say, "Jimmy, what I hear you saying is you hate Mommy. You're very angry, and Mommy makes you sick." Of course not. Jimmy has violated respect for you, and you bring this particular conversation to a halt. "Young man, that's enough. When you can calm down, apologize, and talk to me in a reasonable way, we will continue this conversation."

It's very tough to reflect with angry kids. They're emotionally intense. They fight dirty. They know your weaknesses and will deliberately say things to inflame you. Look, your kids really don't want to talk with you when they're upset, hurt, or angry. They're masters at getting you to react, and when you do, that ends the conversation. Fool them by listening and reflecting and maybe—just maybe—you'll get a real conversation.

Your daughter comes to you and says, "I failed my math test today." She could say this in a number of different ways. You listen and reflect the proper emotion: "You seem really angry about that," or "You seem depressed, hurt, like you're ready to quit," or "You seem happy and relaxed" (that would not be a good sign).

You table your reaction, and reflect in order to build understanding first. Later, you move to some solution and to your own feelings. Even if your child says something outrageous and obviously not true, reflect first. Your child is much more likely to talk and share and listen if you are listening and reflecting.

Recently I saw a couple who had two daughters, ages ten and six.

They were having tremendous problems with the ten-year-old. They described her as difficult, mouthy, and selfish. I didn't mention this, but the mother was also difficult, mouthy, and selfish. Very often, the kid who drives us nuts is the kid who is most like us. This girl was sulking, whining, and disobedient. These parents couldn't seem to hold a decent conversation with their daughter. After just a few sentences, all three would be yelling and saying all kinds of nasty things they didn't really mean.

The problem was, the parents weren't listening and reflecting. In therapy, I forced them to be quiet and listen to what the girl was saying. Frankly, the kid was difficult to listen to because she had an annoying, whining style of speech. But as they listened, they realized what was really happening. Underneath the mouthy, disobedient exterior was a little girl who felt rejected. She told them she felt her younger sister was being praised more often and with more enthusiasm. She said they expected more from her because she was older and it was hard to please them.

They realized she was right. Because she was the firstborn and a more difficult child, they were being too hard on her. When they acknowledged this to her, their daughter felt understood. They extended the conversation and found out her true feelings and were able to solve the problem—all because they listened and reflected. And because they had a great therapist. (Just kidding.)

When your child is talking, make sure there are no distractions or outside interference of any kind. Establish eye contact. Listen, reflect, and build understanding. Then, only after you have done this and it is your turn, teach your child to listen to you and to feed back what you are saying and feeling. That's good communication. That's one of the ways you build respect.

I've got more communication skills that will help you in meeting your child's need for respect. Take some time to digest what I've shared to this point, and I'll cover these additional skills in the next chapter.

YOUR BATTLE PLAN

1. Describe a child you know (yours or someone else's) who has no respect. What happened to cause this lack of respect?

2. What limits do you allow your children to place on you? Do you respect your child's privacy?

3. How are you at listening to your child and reflecting his/her emotions? Why is this hard for you?

CHAPTER 11

"PLEASE RESPECT ME," PART TWO

WHEN OUR FIRST CHILD, Emily, was born, she came out of the birth canal with a bang. Everyone in the hospital room—in fact, everyone in the maternity wing—knew Emily had arrived because she was yelling her little head off. Right from the start, Sandy and I knew we had a very forceful personage on our hands.

Emily is a physical, energetic, and intense person. She's feisty and opinionated. When she's making a point, she'll often raise her voice and pound her fist on the table. Her rants are legendary.

When our second child, Leeann, was born eighteen months later, we figured she'd be a lot like Emily. Boy, were we wrong. It was like night and day. It was like going from a Metallica heavy-metal concert to a Michael Bublé concert. High intensity to low intensity.

When Leeann came out, she was very quiet and peaceful. We thought something was wrong with her. It was as if she didn't want to bother anyone with her birth.

Leeann is a low-key, easygoing, go-with-the-flow person. She doesn't get upset too often. She has opinions, but doesn't share them in a forceful way. No table pounding for her.

Isn't it amazing how your children are so different? And they enter the world that way. They come out with a distinct personality. That being the case, to build respect, you have to use a communication style that fits each child's personality.

Speak Your Child's Language

Something I've learned over the years is that each of my four children has a natural, chosen style of communication. It's their own unique language. It's how they express themselves. If I really want to connect with them, it makes no sense to use my style of communication. I need to use their styles of communication.

My Emily is a writer. She loves to express herself in writing, and she is good at it. She's always sending friends and family members notes and letters. When she really wants to get a point across, she writes. Guess what I need to do if I really want to get a point across to Emily? That's right. I sit down and write her a note. Since that's her language, it works like a charm. After she reads my note (which could be on paper or in a text), she'll usually respond with a note. We usually end up talking about it, but the main avenue with Emily is the written word.

My Leeann is a talker. She loves to talk and uses a lot of words to express herself. She is a highly verbal person and a very interesting conversationalist. She'll use great detail in describing situations, events, and concerns in her life. No detail is too small for Leeann. She tells long stories, often using word pictures to illustrate her point. When I want to reach Leeann in a conversation, I talk the way she talks. I try to use details, more words, and more pictures. I may describe a movie I've seen or use an elaborate analogy in order to make my point. Leeann appreciates this approach and my messages get across. Of course, I need to make sure I set aside a good twenty minutes because Leeann will respond to my detailed story with one of her own.

My Nancy is a lot like my mother. What that means communication-wise, is that Nancy wastes no words. She is straight-forward, direct, and blunt. When Nancy has something to say, she says it. No frills. No details. No beating around the bush. So when I talk to Nancy, I cut to the chase. I say what I have to say straight out. She'd never tolerate a long, involved story. Life's too short for that. She just wants to get to the point.

My William is a typical guy. Unlike the girls, I can't just sit down and talk with him. If I tried that, I'd lose him after five seconds. He's always moving, always doing something, and he talks and shares himself as he engages in an activity.

When William was growing up, how did I talk to him about things that really mattered? I talked to him in short spurts as we played together. Sometimes I related what I was saying to the sport or activity we were doing. "William, great hit! You didn't stop trying to hit the baseball even though you missed the first ten pitches. It's important to keep trying. Right?"

William took in my message because it was part of an activity. Now that he's an adult, I use the same approach. As we play eighteen holes of golf, I can talk to him about important topics along the way.

Find out your children's styles of communication, and use them. If you use each child's preferred language, your messages will get across, and your kids will open up. It works!

Bedtime Talks

Talk to your kids just before they go to sleep. When it's the end of the day and they're finally winding down, you have a good opportunity to slip a message into their heads and maybe from there to their hearts. Their brain waves are different. Their defenses are down. They're more mellow. You can sit on the edge of the bed or lie down beside them and do some neat connecting. They may also tell you things that they wouldn't have earlier in the day.

Bedtime Prayers

Pray out loud at bedtime. A brief prayer saying some things you want them to hear is a great way to communicate. Don't lay it on too thick. Be subtle and tactful. Because it's directed to God, not to them, they tend to be less defensive; they can take what you pray to heart.

For example, if you're trying to teach forgiveness, you could pray this prayer: "Dear Father, thank You so much for sending Jesus to die for our sins. Thank You for forgiving all of our sins. Help us to forgive those who hurt us."

Don't Break Your Kid

Never belittle your child's looks, abilities, habits, mannerisms, or performance. This is a serious breach of respect. Kids are fragile. They are extremely sensitive. You can literally break them with careless comments and sharp criticism. I've talked to many kids who have suffered deep, lasting wounds from a parent's mouth. They do not recover from verbal assaults easily. There is no place for sarcasm or put-downs. Even if they do it to you, make sure you don't retaliate.

Apology

Let's be honest. We all blow it occasionally in the parenting department. I sure did. Ever spanked the wrong kid? I've done that. I came upon the scene of the crime and made a too-hasty, snap decision. "It's usually you who starts these things. Come over here!" I'd find out later that, for once, the usual instigator was innocent.

Ever yelled at a kid? I've done that. A long day, too much stress, or just tired. Whatever the reason, there was no excuse. Whenever I yelled, my real message never got across.

Ever promised something and not come through? I've done that. It's not pleasant to see the look of hurt and disappointment in a kid's eyes. "But Daddy, you promised!"

What I had to do—and what I urge you to do—was humble myself and walk down the hallway to my child's room. I knocked on the door and entered quietly. I gently and softly said, "Daddy was wrong. I made a mistake. I hurt you, and I'm sorry. Please forgive me."

Then I made the situation right if I could by making a change in the area where I blew it. I'd spank the right kid. I'd work hard not to yell. I'd do what I promised to do.

Parenting is a self-correcting process. Children will almost always forgive you when they see genuine sorrow and real change. If we expect them to be truly sorry and correct their mistakes, we'd better do the same.

Kiss the Lecture Good-bye

Last, you need to realize that children and teens have very brief attention spans. Especially when parents are talking. Give up the lecture as a means of communication. I know it's a shame because some of you are superb lecturers. You slowly build your case. Its logic is airtight. It's nothing less than a work of art. The finest law professor in the world would cry with envy at your oratorical skills. Too bad your kid has tuned you out after the first minute. You're beating your gums for nothing.

Learn to speak in short, clear bursts. Most kids respond well to this approach. There are a few exceptions, but not many. Speaking in a brief, concise way shows respect. It's good communication. Plus, you can use the twenty minutes you would have wasted on a lecture to do something productive or fun. Now, if you have a kid who enjoys your lectures, fine. Go right ahead. I can see your kid with a pen and paper, taking careful notes. "What was point 4, Dad, Mom?"

Let's move on to the third essential need: competence.

YOUR BATTLE PLAN

1. Talk about your children and their different personalities. Identify their individual styles of communication.

2. Which child will be the hardest to communicate with? Why?

3. Are you willing to do bedtime talks and prayers? What will stop you?

4. How often do you verbally belittle your children? Are you too critical and sarcastic? Why do you think you talk this way?

5. Do you sincerely apologize when you make a mistake and hurt one of your children? What stops you from saying, "I'm sorry"?

6. Are you a lecturer? Where did you learn this skill? Are you willing to drop it?

CHAPTER 12

"PLEASE HELP ME BE COMPETENT"

I WILL NEVER FORGET a young man in his mid-twenties whom I saw in therapy a few years back. His family history was a nightmare. Both his parents were alcoholics who never showed any love for, or interest in, him. As far as they were concerned, he was a mistake. "You should never have been born," they told him over and over.

These miserable excuses for parents told him many other vicious, critical things on a regular basis. The verbal abuse my client endured day after day from the mom and dad almost defied description. It was as if they systematically set out to destroy him. He could never please them. He was always a miserable failure in their eyes. They hated him, and he knew it.

By the time he reached elementary school, he had been stripped of his self-esteem. He hated himself just as much as his parents hated him. He was a very depressed, shy child who had no friends. He didn't have the courage to make friends. He was sure others would reject him. He had serious suicidal thoughts, and was on the verge of killing himself. He believed he had no reason to live.

It was at his lowest and most desperate point that something wonderful happened, something completely unexpected. Something that literally saved his life. A teacher recognized his musical ability and encouraged him to sing. The teacher saw what no one else had seen. This boy had talent in his voice. She arranged voice lessons, got him into several chorus groups, and pushed him to sing solos at school and her church.

As he told me about his teacher, tears streamed down his face. He was so grateful to her for giving him the gift of recognizing his musical ability. His singing became the central focus of his life. It gave him confidence and self-esteem that he'd never had. His parents didn't change. In fact, they continued to attack him verbally until he finally left home at the end of high school. But their power to destroy him was gone. He could sing and they couldn't take that from him.

The only thing that kept this young man alive was his skill in singing. Even though he had nothing else that was positive in his life, his competence in music was enough to sustain him. Every child needs an area of competence.

Definition

I define competence this way: an ability or skill. It means being good at something.

All children are asking themselves, "What am I good at? What can I really excel at?" It is absolutely vital that they find an answer. Your job as a parent is to help your kids answer this question and find something they can do well. If you fail to find your children a skill, their confidence and identity will suffer. They will be much more likely to make mistakes that will cripple and damage their lives.

The Best Anti-Sin Program

In my practice I see a lot of kids who are lazy, unmotivated. They're not putting forth much effort in school, in their activities, or in their spiritual lives. These kids are just coasting through life with an "I don't care" attitude. Their frustrated parents tell me their kids just aren't achieving their full potential. Most of these kids are lazy because they have no area of competence. They're not good at anything, so they have no confidence. They're scared to fail, so they don't try.

I'll tell you what I tell their parents: You must find your child a skill and find it as quickly as you can. When your kid has a skill, he automatically has confidence in himself. This confidence is infectious and will spread to the other areas of his life. It will give him the courage to try hard in areas of weakness. "I'm good at baseball, so I can try at math. Even if I don't do well at math, that's okay, because I'm a good baseball player."

You see how it works? When a kid can do something well—almost anything at all—he feeds off that strength. He now has the intestinal fortitude—the guts—to give other life experiences his best shot.

Kids who act out, get addicted, get pulled into crime, or get stuck in some other area of sin, often have not found an area of competence. It's easy to be good at drinking, drugs, stealing, sex, cheating, gambling . . . If your kid doesn't find an area of positive competence, he'll find an area of negative competence. I guarantee it. Your kid will find something he's good at, something he can use to draw attention and approval from peers. You'd better make sure it's something positive.

I ask the kids who come to my office, "What are you good at?"
Here are the answers I get:

- "I go to the mall."
- "I hang out with my friends."

PARENTING IS HARD AND THEN YOU DIE

- "I text, tweet, Instagram, Facebook, and Snapchat."
- "I listen to music."
- "I watch TV."
- "I play computer games."

These are not areas of competence! If these kids aren't already involved in some area of sinful competence, they soon may be. The best anti-sin program I know is finding kids an area of competence. When they're good at a healthy activity, they don't need to be good at a sinful activity. Kids who discover a skill also discover motivation to work hard, protection from temptation, and a basis of healthy identity for life.

Every Kid Has a Talent

Tell your child that she has an ability. You never, ever waver in your confidence that there is an area in which she will excel. You might begin to wonder in your own mind, because the find-a-skill process takes longer with some kids. But you don't say, "Well, Susie, it doesn't look good. I'm not sure if you're good at anything." No! Here's what you say: "You've got an ability, Susie. I know it. We just have to find it."

God gives every person talents and gifts. In fact, at the point of becoming a Christian, each person receives a spiritual gift (1 Corinthians 12). We are also given human abilities, and it is our responsibility to use these abilities in the service of Christ (1 Peter 4:10-11). Your kid may doubt you when you say she has abilities. Direct her to the Bible. Then it's not you saying it, it's God who is saying it.

Go Ahead, Be Pushy

Find areas of interest and enjoyment, and push for involvement. There are times when it's necessary to push your kid, and this is one of them. If your child likes something, it just might lead to a skill.

I'll never forget how my cruel, heartless parents pushed me into Little League baseball. I liked baseball, so they signed me up on the Dodgers. On the way to my first practice, I got cold feet and told my mom I'd changed my mind. She said, "You'll be fine, kiddo." She stopped our big Vista Cruiser station wagon at the practice field, pushed me out the door, and drove off in a cloud of dust. I was left standing there, holding my cap and glove. I didn't like my mother at that moment. Ten minutes later, I was having the time of my life. I learned how to play baseball, got to know a lot of guys my age, and had a great two years in Little League. All because my parents pushed me.

There are many activities you can push your kid into. Sports are a great avenue to skills. There are school teams and city leagues. Maybe your kid enjoys golf, tennis, or martial arts. There are hobbies of all sorts: mechanics, woodworking, sewing, computers, crafts, etc.

Look for interest in school subjects like math, science, literature, history, languages, and many more. Work with teachers and come up with creative ways to encourage your child to learn more in his favorite subject. You can sample the variety of extracurricular activities and clubs: scouting, music, drama, horseback riding, and dancing.

Every single kid must be involved in some area of interest. Don't overinvolve her, but she needs at least one interest. Let the kid choose, but she must choose something. Give it a decent trial, at least two months, to see if things will click. If it doesn't pan out, choose another activity and try again. It is completely unacceptable to allow a child to come home from school and do nothing except eat, watch television, do social media, and goof off. That is being a slug, and slugs find other slugs to hang out with, and they eventually get into trouble.

Sandy and I gave feedback whenever we saw a skill or a possible skill. But we were low-key. We didn't gush all over our kids. We didn't want to apply too much pressure by being too interested in their being good at a particular activity.

We pushed Emily in singing, drama, and writing. Leeann had (and still has) real ability in playing the piano and drawing. We encouraged Nancy to develop her skills in organization and tennis. We pushed Will to practice his talent at golf, tennis, and basketball.

The Total Truth

A major part of competence is knowing yourself. Your child needs to know who he is—strengths, weaknesses, blind spots, and personality traits—to be confident and have healthy self-esteem. How can he feel good about someone he doesn't know?

To help your child paint this accurate self-portrait, you must consistently give her the truth about herself in all areas. Across the board. I've already covered the importance of feedback concerning skills and abilities. Just be realistic. Don't lie or exaggerate. If she can't sing, she can't sing! I've seen parents encourage their child to be a soloist when it's painfully obvious she doesn't have the pipes.

This accurate view of self includes weaknesses. Your child has weaknesses and must learn how to deal with them. Handle these areas very carefully and in private. Say, "That's not one of your strong points, Bobby."

Some weaknesses, like in a particular sport, don't need to be worked on or corrected. You'll just direct your child to a sport or activity in which he can enjoy success. Other weak areas, like personality traits, will need to be addressed. Character is important, so you'll work with your child to help him be aware of, and change, negative aspects of his personality.

Networking for Your Kid

Have other adults in your child's life also provide feedback on abilities and personal qualities: family members, friends, teachers, coaches, pastors, and youth leaders. Ask these persons to communicate directly to your child the positive qualities they observe. They can do it verbally or in writing.

I can remember the personal notes my private schoolteachers wrote to me at the end of each grading period. It was school policy, and I'm glad it was. I couldn't wait to read those notes! I devoured them. My teachers commented on my academic work and my personality. The praise I received for my self-discipline, sense of humor, and writing ability helped shape my life.

Encouraging other adults to reinforce your child's positive qualities adds a powerful dimension to your program of building Christlike character. These persons see parts of your child that you don't see. In the case of teachers, they may spend more time with your kid than you do.

Also, feedback packs more punch when it comes from someone else. Kids, especially teenagers, tend to discount what parents say. Teens think you really don't know them, you're wrong most of the time, and, "Oh, you're my parent. You're supposed to say that." When other adults make comments to teens, they sit up and take notice.

Next, we'll zero in on the one need that will have the most impact on your child's life.

YOUR BATTLE PLAN

1. How did your parents do in helping you find your areas of competence? How did you find out what you were good at?

2. What are your children's areas of interest and enjoyment?

3. What will stop you from pushing your children to be involved in activities they're interested in?

4. What adults in your children's life can provide direct feedback on their abilities and personal qualities? Are you willing to ask these adults to give your children regular positive feedback?

CHAPTER 13

"PLEASE HELP ME GROW IN CHRIST"

IT'S NOT EASY being a little kid. You're small and everyone else is big. The world is a scary place. You have no power, no say over your life, and you are totally dependent on others.

Elementary school is tough. You learn how to make friends, get along with teachers, and do homework. You find out some academic subjects are very difficult to understand. You discover you have weaknesses and limitations.

Middle school is . . . well, middle school. In a word, brutal. You are extremely self-conscious and sensitive to the slightest hint of criticism. You realize your parents aren't perfect. In fact, you think your parents are clueless wonders who don't know anything. You try to find out what you're good at and who you are.

High school is no picnic. You have more freedom, but also much more responsibility. You make important decisions about friends, lifestyle, values, and your future. You distance yourself from your parents as you struggle to become an independent person.

Add to all these challenges the state of our culture. It is not disintegrating; it has disintegrated. Pornography on demand and absolutely free. Alcohol and drugs everywhere. Marijuana being legalized in state after state. Racial tensions exploding. Our country more divided politically than ever before. The main role models for our children are spoiled sports stars, worldly musicians and actors, and moronic reality-show stars.

Your child also must deal with a supernatural bad guy with tremendous power and cunning. This bad guy's name is Satan. Satan is real and he hates your kid's guts. He's got a picture of your kid tacked up on the bulletin board in hell. He's holding regular strategy meetings on how to get to your kid.

If Satan can't have your kid's soul, he'll settle for whatever damage he can do in his life. He knows your kid's weaknesses and he'll attack at these vulnerable points. Satan loves to go after kids because he has the opportunity to put into place sinful, destructive patterns that can last a lifetime.

Read the chilling words in 1 Peter 5:8: "Be sober-minded; be watchful. Your adversary the devil prowls around like a roaring lion, seeking someone to devour."

Your Child Needs a Superhero

What if your child could build a close relationship with a superhero? A real, literal superhero with all the power in the universe. A superhero who will protect her, guide her, and teach her. Who will give her strength to resist temptation and make good choices. Who will give her purpose and meaning in her life.

This superhero is God. Your child can have a close bond with God and get His help to grow up in a healthy, successful way.

The first step in meeting the need of spirituality is leading your child to God through Jesus Christ. In chapter 1, I explained how to do this. Once your child knows Jesus, she knows God and can begin to grow spiritually.

Definition

I define spirituality this way: to know Christ and to grow in Christ.

As your child grows closer to Jesus Christ, she will grow closer to God. God, through Jesus, will give her the ability to become a person who glorifies God with her life.

Here's how to help your child grow in Christ.

Model a Godly Lifestyle

My dad, Bill Clarke, is the most godly man I know. He repeatedly told my brother, Mark, and me: "Guys, there is nothing more important in life than a vital, growing relationship with Jesus Christ." My dad didn't just say it. He took action to make it happen in our lives.

So do what my dad did in two critical areas.

Daily Personal Quiet Time with God

One of the vivid memories etched in my mind is of my dad in his chair in the family room, every morning of my life, having his devotions. He had the Bible open, plus a few other books—Bible study aids, devotional guides, etc. Every morning, without fail, I could count on Dad doing his devotions like the sun coming up. Even when I got up at different times—weekends, holidays—Dad would be there.

Years later, when I was an adult, I told my dad, "It was so strange that every morning, no matter when I got up, I'd see you having your quiet time with God." Dad said, "Dave, there was nothing strange about it. I made sure you saw me having my time with God."

Teach Your Kids How to Have a Quiet Time

The second action my dad took was to teach me how to have my own personal quiet time. For five days, he invited me into his time with God. He showed me how to pray, using the ACTS formula: *adoration* of God, *confession* of my sins, *thanking* God for what He's done for me, and *supplication* (a fancy term for making my prayer requests).

After prayer, he demonstrated how to read a brief devotional, read a short passage in the Bible, and meditate for a few minutes on the passage.

I still follow these same steps in my quiet time with God! And I taught each of my four kids the same steps.

Once-a-Week Family Devotions

As our kids grew up, I led a family devotions time once a week. It was very simple: four steps, twenty minutes tops, and we were done.

One: Going around the circle, I'd check in with each child. The kids had a chance to talk about anything going on in their lives and any concerns or problems they were facing—in and outside the family.

Two: One child would read out loud the short Bible passage I had selected.

Three: I'd teach the passage's principle and then apply it to my life and the lives of each child.

Four: We'd end with prayer. I'd ask for prayer requests, then each person would pray for the person seated to the right of them.

If there's a dad in the home, it's his job to lead the family devotions. If there's no dad, or he won't do it, the mom will have to lead.

Keep Your Kids in Church

Find a church with an excellent children's program and an excellent youth program. They will get great modeling and teaching from the adult leaders. They will make friends with other quality kids. And, they will have many fun, safe, and spiritual activities to go to.

Do what Sandy and I did. We told our kids that as long as they lived in our home, they would go to church. They would attend Sunday morning and go to all the activities for children and youth during the week. No excuses. It was the law.

Help Your Kid Be Like Christ

One of the essential functions parents have is developing character in their children. Specifically, Christlike character. It's vital that children see themselves as being like Christ. The good news is, we parents can create character in our kids. One of the ways we can do this is to reinforce Christlike behavior when we see it.

One time, we were all sitting at the dining room table at the start of supper. I cut my prayer short because Sandy had made sourdough rolls. I love sourdough rolls. I would kill for sourdough rolls. Anyway, the sourdough rolls began their trip around the table. With four kids, it took a while. My anticipation grew as the basket approached the end of the table, where Emily and I were sitting. Emily took the basket, lifted the cloth, and paused. I was horrified to see that there was only one roll left! I couldn't believe it. Sandy had apparently made only five sourdough rolls. What kind of game was she playing?

It was an awkward moment. Then Emily, sweet Emily, said, "Dad, go ahead. You can take the last roll. I know you like sourdough rolls." I didn't waste any time. I grabbed that roll, and said, "Thanks, Emily. That was very kind." Later that evening, just before bed, I made it a point to thank Emily again for her act of kindness. I told her she was like Christ in being a kind, thoughtful servant.

Sandy told me later, "You know, you could have broken the roll in half and shared it with Emily."

I said, "Yeah, I could have. But I wanted to give Emily a chance to be like Christ." Actually, that didn't dawn on me. I just wanted that roll. I was being kind—like Christ—because I didn't say to Sandy what I wanted to say: "You should have made six rolls."

As I did with Emily, look for situations in which your kids display positive and Christlike qualities. Catch them being like Christ and verbally stroke them.

- "You're friendly."
- "You're sensitive to the needs of others."
- "You speak the truth."
- "You're kind."
- "You didn't quit."
- "You chose to forgive."
- "You shared with your sister."
- "You read the Bible."
- "You love Jesus and it shows."

Your children will take your objective feedback and use it to form their identities. Step by step, positive reinforcement by positive reinforcement, you will help mold them into being like Christ.

Four needs down, one to go. This last need will, to a large extent, determine if you will be a successful parent.

YOUR BATTLE PLAN

1. What part of your childhood was the most difficult? Why?

2. Do each of your children have a personal relationship with God through Jesus Christ? If not, read chapter 1 again and consider explaining to each child how to begin a relationship with Him. Or talk to one of your pastors and ask him/her to meet with each child.

3. Are you having a daily personal quiet time with God? If not, why not? If you are, do your children know you are doing this?

4. Are you willing to teach your kids how to have a daily quiet time with God? What would stop you from doing this?

5. What will be challenging about leading a weekly family devotional?

6. Are you regularly attending a church with excellent programs for children and youth? Do you require your kids to attend church and these programs?

7. Are you willing to verbally reinforce Christlike behavior in your children?

CHAPTER 14

"PLEASE LET ME GO"

ONE OF THE MOST pathetic sights I see in counseling is the dependent young adult. He has not achieved independence from his parents. He can't make it in the world on his own. He still relies heavily on his parents for emotional and perhaps even financial support. Often, he still lives at home.

I am seeing more and more Millennials who are unable or unwilling to live independently of their parents. These young adults will go away to college, but then come back home and never leave. Or take years to leave.

Definition

I define independence this way: living on your own, paying all your own bills, and being responsible for all the decisions that guide your life.

By helping your child achieve independence, you do three very important things. First, you meet the last need required to build a successful, godly person.

Second, you fulfill your ultimate goal as a parent: *getting rid of your kids*! I mean, launching them into the world.

Third, you get the kids out of the house so you can have some fun! It's your turn, baby! If your kids leave your home and stay gone, you have freedom again! You have time again! You have money again! Remember money? You have a life again!

Can I get an "amen" from the parents reading this? Thank you. Sandy and I understand. We are on the verge, the cusp of empty-nesterhood. We have one more kid to move out and we will attain parental nirvana.

To make sure your children achieve independence, follow these steps.

Teach Them to Make Their Own Decisions

Allow your children to make their own decisions whenever possible. If it isn't a critical area—life or death—let them decide:

- which clothes they buy and wear
- which activities they want to do on the weekend
- which friends they hang out with and invite to your home
- what they choose to order in a restaurant

With younger kids, offer them choices. "Do you want to wear this outfit or that one?" "Do you want to clean up your toys or set the table?"

In these noncritical areas, use language that encourages independence:

- "The choice is yours."
- "You decide about that."

- "It's your decision."
- "It's up to you."
- "Do what you believe you should do."
- "Think about it, then make the call."

When you talk this way, you build your children's confidence in their ability to make decisions. You send the message: "You're a sharp kid, and we know you are capable of making good choices in life." Make sure they realize they'll make mistakes. Everybody does. That's part of the learning process in life.

Force your kids to wrestle with tough decisions. When your kids come to you with problems and sticky situations, don't immediately give them an answer. Even if you're right, they don't learn anything. They don't learn to think for themselves.

I have clients whose parents fed them answers all through childhood. When life got rough, they'd run to Mommy and Daddy and get the solution. Now these clients are incredibly indecisive. They're totally paralyzed when faced with decisions. They'll call twenty persons, get advice from each, and still not know what to do.

When your kids approach you with issues, always ask them, "What do you think?" Make them struggle with the situation out loud and think their way through it. Give your input, but only after they have used their own brain cells to arrive at a decision. If it isn't a vital area, let them go ahead with their decision. Even if it's a mistake. Some of life's most important lessons are learned from mistakes.

Show your kids how you make decisions. No one else is going to teach them how. That's your job. Let them see you listing the pros and cons, praying, reading the Bible, talking to your spouse, talking to family members and good friends, and getting counsel from trusted persons. Too many parents keep their decision making a secret. These parents tell me, "We don't want to scare our kids or make them insecure." My response is, "If you don't show them how to make decisions now, they'll be scared and insecure when they hit the real world."

Whatever skill you don't teach your kids is a skill they won't have when they're adults.

Push Them Out of the Nest

Your kids will not become independent unless you push them into healthy activities away from home. Don't let them become too comfortable at home, because they won't be living there forever. Sleepovers ought to begin in second grade. Unless your child has a bona fide emergency or some extraordinary crisis, make her stay the night. If a little whining brings Mom or Dad running to rescue her, she may never complete a sleepover.

I'm a big believer in Christian summer camps. Check out the camp and the leaders carefully. Because your kids will be out of your care for at least one week, you must demand the highest possible caliber of Christianity in the camp administration and counselors. Sandy and I have been delighted with Camp Cedarbrook here in Florida. Some of the finest Christians we've ever met run this ministry. Our kids have had fun, matured in many areas, and grown spiritually as a result of their camp experiences.

Church youth outings and events are a part of building independence in your kids. If they don't want to go, tough. Hear them out, listen and reflect, then tell them to get in the car. School activities and sports are a good social outlet and foster independence.

At fifteen or sixteen years of age, a part-time job is a possibility. The job must be earned with good grades and good behavior. Also, the hours must be limited. Any more than ten to twelve hours a week is a mistake. It will lead to fatigue, lower grades, and a reduced social life.

Teach Them Money Management

You can't live without money. And you can't live too well if you don't know how to handle your money. Frankly, this was a weak area of my life until my mid-twenties. Just to prove my parents weren't perfect, they didn't teach me a great deal about money. Looking back, they were probably too generous. I had to learn the nuts and bolts of money management as an adult.

To prepare your kids for the financial realities of life, model careful budgeting and use of your money. Show them the bills. Show them your budget. Tell them how much you make each month, and how much you spend. Teach them how to balance a checkbook. At least by the end of middle school, your kids ought to have a firm grasp on these money skills.

Model tithing to the church and other Christian ministries. Make it clear that all your money is God's money. He has provided it to meet your needs. It's only right and biblical to give back a portion of what God has given so generously. If you want your kids to give to God, let them see you doing it.

Pay your kids for certain jobs they do around the home. When they have some money, you can teach them how to manage it. I like this approach: spend, save, and share—the three *s*'s (this is not original with me). Your kids can spend a certain percentage of their money, save a certain percentage, and share a certain percentage with the Lord.

Teach Basic Living Skills

Before your kids leave home, you need to train them in some humdrum but fundamental areas. They need to know how to do basic household cleaning. The magic genie (or Mom) will not clean their toilets for them when they're living in their own places. They've got to learn how to cook. Boys *and* girls! I'm not talking about gourmet meals. Just simple, hearty fare. They need to be able to do their own laundry. By age twelve your kids should be doing some of their own laundry every week.

And one other thing: Kids must master the skill of taking care of a car. This is especially important with the old rattletraps they'll be driving for a while. Understanding the way an engine works, changing the oil regularly, and doing regular maintenance will save them thousands of dollars.

The Law of the Playground

The world is a nasty place. You know that. And it's getting nastier all the time. And nowhere is it nastier than in your child's world. The deterioration of culture and the breakdown of the family are producing more and more problem kids. There are a lot of bullies, creeps, and just plain mean kids out there. They enjoy teasing, taunting, and physically beating up other children.

These vicious juvenile delinquents are everywhere: public schools, Christian schools, churches, day care centers, and neighborhoods. I'm not talking just about boys. Girls can be incredibly catty and brutal. Your child will come into contact with these kids. Guaranteed. The only question is: How will your child deal with these bullies?

Parents, you've got to get your kids ready to meet the punks of this world. All kids need to be prepared, but there are certain categories of children who are in particular need of anti-punk training: only children, sensitive children, passive children, shy children, children with disabilities, children with speech problems, and children who haven't had much exposure to kids of the same sex. These kids need to be toughened up so they can deal effectively with the attacks of their peers.

You've already read part of my program for preparation. Meeting the four needs I've covered up to now—love, respect, competence, and spirituality—will toughen your kids and give them a healthy level of confidence. Here are some more ideas.

First, let siblings tease each other, and do not intervene unless it gets out of hand. Good old, run-of-the-mill teasing helps your kids build up tolerance. It's good practice for the real thing. So let your kids learn how to take it and dish it out in interactions with their brothers and sisters. If you protect your children from these family attacks, you'll create a bunch of Little Lord Fauntleroys. They'll be cut to ribbons out there where it's really tough.

Second, expose your kids to peers of the same sex in the neighborhood, at school, and in church. These days, it's important to get your children used to interacting with peers at a young age. The more social skills your children have before they hit school, the better.

Third, talk specifically to your kids about what they're going to face. They're going into battle and they might as well know it. Discuss the broad range of possible verbal insults—body characteristics, their name, paternity, family heritage, etc. Develop strategies and role-play situations.

What do you do when your kid is being attacked, verbally or physically, on a regular basis? The bottom line is: Do not allow your child to passively endure vicious teasing or physical bullying. If your child fails to respond, her self-esteem and independence will be seriously wounded. I've had many parents, usually moms, tell me, "But my child should turn the other cheek, like it says in the Bible. Wouldn't Jesus want that?" I reply, "If your child continues to allow bullying, she'll invite more intense bullying. She could be emotionally crippled for life. Would Jesus want that?"

I tell parents that children are like a group of sharks in the ocean. When one of them bleeds, they all attack without mercy until there's nothing left of the victim. The sad reality is, even the good, decent kids join in the massacre. That's not right. That's not fair. But that's the way it is.

I believe there is a place for assertiveness in the lives of Christian adults and kids. Ephesians 4:26 instructs us: "Be angry and do not sin." Let's look at some practical ways you can teach your child to be angry, stop the bullying, and not sin in the process.

Teach Them to Stand Up to Bullies

Step 1 is to stay out of it. It's the absolute kiss of death to have Mommy or Daddy directly intervene. It won't stop the bullying, and it will humiliate your child. Unless there is a clear threat of serious physical harm, just work with your child behind the scenes.

Step 2 is to teach your child to show no weakness. This will be tough if your kid is the sensitive type, but it's critical to success. Practice and role-play until your kid can stare back at you and show no visible response. He or she has to fake a calm exterior and stuff all feelings. When your kid comes home, he can pour out his heart and cry and be as pitiful as he wants to be. But not in front of the bully. That is no place for honest expression. "You've hurt my feelings, Bubba." No! That's what Bubba and all bullies want: a reaction.

Step 3 is to train your child in the art of verbal comebacks. Ignoring insults usually doesn't work. Your child can try it, but don't get your hopes up. What usually does work is calm, witty, sometimes humorous, and sarcastic replies to the bully's taunts. You don't recommend any foul language or vicious retorts. That wouldn't be Christlike. Help your child come up with a collection of memorized comebacks that will make him more of a challenge to the bully. Bullies like easy marks and don't typically have the stomach for a prolonged match of wits. They don't want to risk looking bad in front of their peers. Check with other parents to find some good, contemporary comebacks. Have your kid ask his friends for some material. "Your mother wears army boots" probably won't work in this day and age. Again, role-play until your kid can zing you back with his snappy one-liners. Here are some verbal comebacks that your child can use:

- "You must be really insecure."
- "You don't like yourself, do you?"
- "I wonder why you don't pick on someone bigger and tougher than you?"
- "You're on your way to becoming a criminal."
- "Verbal abuse always comes from jealousy—Google it."
- "I'm recording you right now—keep going."

Step 4 is to advise your kid to get some support from friends. If even one kid will agree to back him up, chances are better the bully will back off. It's harder to pick on two kids. If your child's friend has a smart mouth and is good at verbal jousting, so much the better. In fact, the steps I've suggested are designed to play to the crowd. If your child's responses impress even a few of the onlookers, the bully is in trouble. When the bully senses a loss of even a little crowd support, he'll move on to another kid.

Step 5 is the judicious use of retaliatory physical measures. In other words, there may come a time when your child has to throw a punch. You make it clear that your child is to strike back only in self-defense. He is never to throw the first punch. I taught my kids that if any kid hit them, they were allowed to hit back to protect themselves. I did not want one of my kids to be beaten like a drum and not respond. Sometimes a physical confrontation cannot be avoided. Even if your kid loses the fight, at least he goes down swinging. That may make him too tough an opponent for the bully. And it will win him some respect and support from the ringside crowd.

Any child who will not fight in self-defense can expect to get beaten up every day for the rest of their school years.

On her first day of kindergarten, our daughter Nancy was confronted by a bully. We thought she would be safe at this nice, Christian, church-based school. We were wrong. No child is safe from bullying in any school. But we had taught her that it was okay to defend herself. At recess that day, a boy in her class thought he could intimidate her. Nancy was the smallest kid in the class. He threw sand at her in the sandbox. Nancy immediately threw sand in his face. The little punk cried his eyes out and ran to the teacher. He did not bother her the rest of the year. And neither did any other kid in her class.

Sandy and I gave Nancy a couple of high fives and congratulated her on how she handled this bully. The entire class got the message that day: "Don't mess with Nancy Clarke."

One final point. When a bully tells your kid to meet him after school for a fight, there is only one good response: "No, let's do it right now." The bully wants to get mileage all day out of his challenge. He wants your kid to suffer in anguish for hours. But most of all, he wants no school officials around to stop the fight and punish him. When your kid forces the bully to fight immediately, it ensures that the fight won't go the distance. If a teacher shows up, the bully may get in trouble. Plus, your kid earns some respect from other peers.

Okay, you've got your Parenting Team in place and you understand how to meet these five critical needs in the lives of your children. Now you're ready for my practical, hands-on, proven system of discipline. This system raised our four Clarkes to be great persons. It will do the same for your kids.

YOUR BATTLE PLAN

1. What struggles did you have in becoming an independent person? How could your parents have done a better job meeting your need for independence?

2. Are you allowing your kids to make their own decisions? What's hard about this?

3. Are you pushing your kids into healthy activities away from home? If you struggle in this area, why?

4. How are you doing teaching your kids money management? What can you do to improve?

5. Are you teaching your kids basic living skills (cleaning, cooking, laundry, taking care of a car)?

6. What's your reaction to my anti-bullying plan? What will stop you from getting your children tough and ready to deal with bullies?

PART THREE

Discipline

CHAPTER 15

DISCIPLINE THAT WORKS

You're at the mall with your children. It's just you and them—no spouse. You've just said no to your little boy. Without warning, he suddenly throws himself to the floor and launches into a full-blown tantrum. I mean, this tantrum has it all: yelling and screaming, foaming at the mouth, legs and arms thrashing, and the little back arched. If it weren't so annoying, you'd be impressed with his acrobatic ability. But it is annoying . . . and embarrassing.

You see disapproving looks from several bystanders, and you get the distinct impression that they blame you for your son's behavior. You lean down to grab his arm, he jerks up suddenly, and his head connects with your head. Your head is ringing, your arms are full of bags, and you want to spank Timmy so badly you can taste it. It's ten miles to the parking lot. What do you do?

Here's another example. It's bedtime at your home. At last! It's been a long day and even though you love your kids, you've had about enough. You want peace and quiet, and some time for yourself. You want your kids to go to bed, go to sleep, and leave you alone. That's the dream.

The reality is, you have one child who won't go to bed. Tonight, like most nights, she fights bedtime tooth and nail. She keeps dragging out of her room with the same ridiculous excuses: "I'm thinking bad thoughts." "I need water"—which, of course, is followed five minutes later by "I have to go to the bathroom." Oh, what a shocker! "I heard a strange noise." And the classic: "It's too dark in here." You say, "Funny thing, honey, it gets dark every night about this same time."

You try all the same ridiculous solutions: reasoning with her, threatening her, and begging her. You turn off all the lights. You lie down next to her in bed, which puts you to sleep, not her. You play music. If you hear one more song, you'll scream. Nothing works. It's 8:30 . . . 9:00 . . . 9:30, and another evening is shot. How do you get the kid to bed?

All right, here's yet another scene. Your thirteen-year-old daughter has just finished another one of her screaming, crying, whining tirades. All you did was ask her to get off the phone because an hour and a half was enough time to talk and text. She didn't take it well. She said she hated you, that you didn't love her, and that you weren't "cool" like Cindy's mom. According to her, living with you is like being in a concentration camp. Your sweet, kind, obedient daughter has turned into a teenage werewolf.

Ever since her thirteenth birthday, it's like an alien has invaded her body. She's angry, disrespectful, selfish, critical, and lies like a rug. At least she isn't moody—she has only one mood: bad. She doesn't want much. Just complete freedom, all your money, and everything her way. What do you do with a teenager like this? (And most of them are like this.)

The Solution Is Discipline

These are just three scenes. I could go on and on. I have four kids, and I have worked with a lot of parents and kids. All of us as parents have unpleasant stories like these, don't we? The problem in each one of these stories is a child:

- testing a parent
- challenging authority
- seeing how far he can go to get his way

The solution is discipline. Solid, healthy, balanced discipline. Discipline is the painful process of teaching children limits.

We must teach discipline because it leads to self-control, patience, character, respect, and accomplishment. Our children need these qualities to have a successful life.

We also teach discipline for ourselves, because if we don't, our children will make our lives a living nightmare. There's no end to the pain and damage undisciplined kids can wreak on our lives. To be sure, I don't have all the answers in the area of discipline. But I do have a training program—a strategy—that I believe will help you. My strategy begins with the three prerequisites for effective discipline. You must understand these three things first to have any chance of being an effective disciplinarian.

1. Your Children Need to Rebel

That's right, you read those words correctly. Rebellion is a healthy, normal, and important part of becoming one's own person, breaking away, and achieving independence. Your children won't become independent unless they rebel. You're thinking, "You're saying we can't stop it?" That's what I'm saying. The key is to allow rebellion in minor areas, not major areas.

In my opinion, here are some minor areas. Hair is minor. Believe me. Let them wear their hair the way they want. It's really not a big deal. Some parents think long hair is one step away from drug use. It's not! It's just long hair.

The clothes your kids wear are also not something to have a fit about. Within reason, let them wear the clothes they want to wear. As long as their clothes are not too revealing or outrageous, let them make a statement. There's no harm in this kind of "rebellion."

Every peer group has an approved dress code. If your kids don't wear those clothes, they don't make it in. Fair? No. Reality? Oh yeah. Your kids know the dress code. You don't, because you're old.

And food. Don't force them to eat their vegetables. Don't force them to clean their plates. They'll eat when they're hungry. Very few kids starve to death. Now, if they choose not to eat the good food, there is a small price to pay. They can't have snacks or dessert.

I'm about to break a lot of hearts. Their rooms are also a minor area. Please stop trying to make your kids clean their rooms. Oh, the vicious, pitched battles I've seen over the condition of their rooms! It's not worth it! Let them revel in their own filth, disorder, and clutter! It's a safe expression of rebellion. Let it go, like releasing a dove to the heavens. Now, if you see a rat squeezing out the door of the room, you may have a real problem. If men in those white, environmental suits come to your front door, you'll know you'll probably have to take steps.

You know what your kids are doing with their messy, nasty room? They're sticking it to the man! Who's the man? You're the man! Again, no big deal. It's a safe—though annoying—expression of rebellion.

If you win in these areas, your kids will rebel in other, major areas. I've seen a lot of acting-out kids whose hair is short and whose rooms are clean and tidy. They've simply moved on to dangerous areas of rebellion. Would you rather have your kids rebel with a messy room or by getting involved in drugs or sex? That could very well be your choice!

Major areas of rebellion are alcohol, drugs, sex, breaking laws, lying, disrespect, and hanging out with dangerous kids. You fight these battles with all you've got, because these behaviors can destroy your child. I urge zero tolerance in these areas. Prioritize and fight only the battles that are worth fighting. If you respond to every behavior you disagree with, you'll be a basket case! And your kid will rebel big-time in the big areas.

2. You Cannot Control Your Children's Behavior

You are doomed to lose the war for control over their behavior. You can't control the behavior of any other person! Think about it. Can you control your spouse's behavior? Of course not. I hope you've stopped trying. How about your boss's behavior? Your best friend's behavior? Your next-door neighbor's behavior? No, no, and no.

Your children can do whatever they want. Whatever they choose. Your job is to teach your children control of their own behavior by applying rewards and consequences after their chosen behavior. I'm going to show you how to do this.

3. You Should Focus on Behavior, Not Attitude

Studies have shown that 99.9 percent of children from 0 to 21 years of age have rotten attitudes. They are, to be politically correct, attitude-challenged. Every now and then you come across a kid with a genuinely good attitude. A real sweetheart. It's like a white rhino—it's extremely rare. Parents, most of you are going to have to put up with:

- the curled lip
- the pouting
- the whining
- the sarcasm

- the body language
- the mean looks

Kids can communicate so much with just a look, can't they? "I hate you." "You're so stupid." "Life has passed you by, Old-timer." "I couldn't care less." Don't let disrespect, profanity, or insults pass without responding. There must be consequences for them.

But you need to allow the basic, garden-variety bad attitude. It's impossible to get rid of a bad attitude, short of brain surgery. That's messy, expensive, and your insurance won't cover it. It is possible to help them improve their behavior. And that's just what my discipline strategy will help you do.

A Strategy for War

You need a strategy, because if you wing it in discipline, you'll get run over repeatedly by your kids. You'll have tire tracks and sneaker prints all over your back. You're in a war, my friends—a nasty guerrilla war. You have to be smart, on your toes, because you're up against a worthy opponent. Children are clever and committed to their cause. They want fun and freedom, and you're in the way.

Kids lie awake at night figuring out how to outwit you. They have the energy and the free time. You do not. Speaking for myself, as a parent I slept the sleep of the exhausted. You can win the war, but only when you have a strategy, a Battle Plan. I have one for you.

Here is my general strategy: You create a reasonable set of behavior standards and apply reasonable rewards or consequences based on your children's behavior. It's a behavior-based system.

The message you send to your children is this: You are free to live as you choose. It is important that you learn how to live responsibly. So we (or I, if you're a single parent) have developed a reasonable

set of behavior standards. If you meet these sta[r]
rewarded. If you choose not to, you will face th[e]

All kids want independence. They're al[w]
to do things my way!" With my system, yo[u]
things your way. But based on your choices, there w[ill]
or consequences." My system is God's system. When we obey [His]
standards in the Bible, He rewards us. When we don't, He applies
consequences.

The goal of this strategy is making the focus the behavior of your
children and the rewards or consequences that they earn. They choose
to be rewarded or choose to earn consequences. It's up to them.

Keep in mind, you cannot control your children's behavior. But
you do control, rigidly, the rewards and consequences you apply. You
must apply rewards and consequences each time, consistently, or the
whole system collapses. Remember: Consistency is as strategic as the
rewards and consequences.

If you're married, work as a team. That's God's Plan A. If you are
a single parent or your spouse refuses to be involved, do it yourself
with the support of family, friends, church, and by praying and trusting God for the courage and strength. This is Plan B, but with God's
help, it will be just as effective as Plan A.

Let's take a closer look at consequences. First, I'll cover consequences for younger kids: birth through kindergarten. Then, I'll
describe consequences for older kids.

YOUR BATTLE PLAN

1. What are the main ways your kids act out? To date, have your
   methods of dealing with their behavior been successful?

2. What was your parents' approach to discipline? Did it work
   with you?

3. Do you allow your children to rebel? If so, in what ways?

.. Do you battle your children over the condition of their rooms? Can you let this minor area go?

5. Do you believe your children's attitude is a big deal? If so, why? Can you overlook their attitude and focus on their behavior?

CHAPTER 16

CONSEQUENCES FOR YOUNGER KIDS

WHILE SHE WAS PREGNANT, a Seattle woman drank up to half a fifth of bourbon a day. As a result, her son was born retarded and malformed. She sued the makers of bourbon for not warning her that she was harming her unborn son.

A woman smoked heavily her entire adult life. She had part of a cancerous lung removed and yet continued to smoke. Her doctors told her if she didn't stop smoking, she'd be dead inside of two years. She kept right on smoking. Inside of two years, she died of cancer. End of story, right? Wrong. Her relatives sued the tobacco company for causing her death.

A man planned a boating trip for the coming weekend. He watched a local twenty-four-hour weather channel to check the conditions. The weather forecast was for smooth seas and clear skies. But while he was on the water, a quick-moving storm came up and the high waves sank his boat. It was a total loss. He was rescued, but he wasn't as grateful as he was angry. He sued the weather channel for not warning him about the storm.

And here's my personal favorite. A young man strapped a refrigerator to his back and walked the course of a local footrace. No one made him do it. It was his own idea. After suffering severe injuries to his back (duh!), he sued the makers of the refrigerator. He said the company had failed to warn him of the potential consequences of carrying their product on his back.

I wish I could say these stories are isolated, ridiculous exceptions to the rule. But I can't. All over the world people are filing lawsuits to take revenge (and get money) for accidents or foolish actions they took! No one seems to be willing to take the blame for their own choices anymore. There is an entire class of people, millions strong, who want to make others pay for their mistakes. My theory is, these individuals had parents who didn't have the courage to apply consequences. When children don't suffer proper punishment for their poor choices, they grow up to be professional victims and blamers.

Do not let this happen to your kids! Kids, by nature, want to avoid paying the price for their bad behavior. They'll lie, cheat, and distort the truth in a desperate attempt to escape consequences. How many times have you asked your kids who committed a particular offense (wrote on the wall, clogged the toilet, called Tokyo on the phone), only to have each one of them say with a straight face, "Not me." You could show your kid a videotape of him calling Tokyo, and he'd still deny it and try to worm his way out of the punishment. Because you love your children and want them to become honest, responsible adults, you must apply consequences after disobedient behavior.

Truth or Consequences

You can use just about anything to punish your children. I want you to feel free, with a few exceptions. Food, water, and shelter are off-limits. I know it can be tempting, but don't use these. You wouldn't say, "Bobby, you're sleeping in the front yard tonight." Also, don't use church time. It's okay to keep them from going to a special youth activity, but not regular, in-church programs. You don't want to hold them back from worshiping God and learning more about Him. Also, I don't recommend withholding individual one-on-one time with a parent as a consequence. This is relationship-building time, and I wouldn't tamper with it.

Spankers of the World, Unite!

Spanking is effective punishment for children who are, roughly, eighteen months to six or seven years old. (It is not for teenagers. Spanking teenagers is humiliating and counterproductive.) My life verse as a young parent was Proverbs 22:15: "Folly is bound up in the heart of a child, but the rod of discipline drives it far from him." Yes! I read that verse and cheer! God says spanking is a valuable tool in discipline, and He hasn't changed His mind.

Spanking is for defiance and willful disobedience. When your child shakes his fist in your face and says, "No, I won't do it!" that's a spanking offense. You'll say, "I will now apply Proverbs 22:15 to your backside." He'll ask, "What's Proverbs 22:15?" You'll reply, as you begin the spanking, "Read your Bible, son."

Spanking is also for protection from danger. The only way I taught little William Clarke not to go into the road in front of our home was spanking. It's a busy road and cars zip by going fast. After the fourth or fifth spanking, William learned it didn't pay to go into the road. If I'd tried to reason with him, he'd be dead now. You can't reason with small kids! They don't know what you're talking about. Don't waste your breath. Spank, and they'll get the message.

The pain of spanking helps break the will. Not the spirit, but the will. You have to break the will of every child—and the sooner, the better. There's nothing quite as ugly as a teenager or young adult with an unbroken will. If you don't break a child's will, she'll break you.

Spanking is done privately. It's not a spectator sport. You don't say, "Gather around, kids. I'm going to spank Susie!" And you are angry when you spank. I know that many experts say, "Never spank a child in anger." And I understand the concern about potential abuse. But of course you're angry! You don't spank when you're in a good mood, do you? "Come here, Susie. Mom's happy, so I think I'll spank you." You're angry, but not in a rage. Sometimes, we all get too angry and are in danger of crossing the line from discipline into abuse. When that happens, back off and cool down. You'll still be angry, but you must also be in control.

Three to five swats are usually enough. Don't spank until the kid cries or begs for mercy. Use your hand or some kind of a paddle. Spank the bottom only. Never should a child ever be struck in any way, on any other part of the body. Leave the child alone, then return to talk.

You want an apology. A real apology—to you, to anyone else the child offended, and to God. You make it clear that disobedience is not just against you, but also against God. A real apology shows a broken will, which is exactly what you want. When the apology is offered, give the child affection. The relationship goes back to normal. If there is no apology, don't spank again. Move right into time-out.

After one of my parenting seminars, one parent told me that she requires a written apology after particularly mean behavior. The child writes out an apology to the parent, any other person involved, and God. Also, the child must include appropriate Scripture that bears on his disobedient act. Then, the child reads the apology out loud to the family. I like that idea. It might be helpful if you're dealing with a strong-willed kid.

If done correctly, spanking will not teach your child to hit others. That is a common liberal view, and it's not true. Now, if you physically abuse your children (hit, punch, kick), that will certainly cause emotional damage, and lead to them hitting others. But if you spank in the controlled way I've described, God's way, then it teaches self-control and obedience.

Time-Out for Acting Out

Time-out is sending your young child (or taking him kicking and screaming, as the case may be) to an environment devoid of any entertainment or pleasure for a period of time. Time-out is typically used for behavior short of outright defiance.

Use a bathroom. The kid's room is too much fun and way too comfortable. In his room, the kid has all his special things: bed, toys, special blanket, iPads, etc. There's nothing to do in a bathroom except go to the bathroom. After that, the kid is just sitting on the pot. Reverse the lock if necessary, to keep the kid inside. Some ornery kids will just come waltzing right out.

Ten minutes is a good rule of thumb. If the kid screams or makes a racket after ten minutes, time is added. "For each minute you scream, I'll double the time you spend in there." The kid could be in there for a while, but you hold the line. If he has to use the bathroom, no problem. He's already there. If he gets thirsty, there's plenty of water in there. "Drink out of the toilet, honey. It doesn't hurt the dog." Food isn't a problem. Just give him food that slips under the door: hot dogs, bread, potato chips. If he's made a mess, he must clean it up before he comes out.

When the time is up, go to the child and talk. Again, as with spanking, you want an apology. No apology, no release from jail. A strong-willed child will refuse to apologize. Fine. When it's bedtime, he'll go from time-out in the bathroom to his room. There will also be serious consequences the next day: more time-out, loss of the use of toys, no videos or television, no playing outside, etc.

A real tough, strong-willed child will not give you the reaction you want. The will of a strong-willed kid is a lot tougher to break than the will of the typical, normal child. Don't expect, or try to get, a penitent reaction. He or she won't give you the satisfaction of showing you true brokenness. "Spank me more—you're not hurting me." Or "I'll sit in this bathroom all week, and you'll never get me to apologize."

Just stay the course and continue to use spanking and time-out. Show no reaction. Eventually, brokenness will take place inside. This kind of kid won't admit any change of heart, but you'll see proof of a broken will in improved behavior.

You spank or use time-out as soon as possible after the misbehavior. This clearly connects the misbehavior to the consequence. The same principle applies to rewards. If you catch your child being good, reward her right away. If the reward isn't soon, small kids will forget what it's for.

Spanking and time-out are effective for younger children because they really have no life. What do you take away from a kid who has nothing? All younger kids do is eat, sleep, go to the bathroom, and bother you! Older kids have more in their lives and you can take what they have, piece by piece. (More on this in the next chapter.)

Shunning Isn't Just for the Amish

Another effective corrective measure is a technique called extinguishing. (No, it has nothing to do with spraying your kid with a fire extinguisher.) This is a fancy name for ignoring behavior you don't like. It's particularly effective for fits, whining, when a kid asks over and over for something, and when a kid goes into that one special mode that drives you insane. He is hateful, angry, hostile, verbally abusive, or all of the above. A kid acts in these ways to get what he wants and to get a reaction from you. And he'll settle for either one.

When your kid moves into that mode, you ignore him. You don't respond. You say nothing. You have no reaction. You go about your business as if nothing is happening. You continue your conversation with your spouse, keep watching television, doing the laundry, reading your book, or cooking the evening meal.

It's just like the Amish and their shunning a member of the community who has broken an important rule. When the kid stops the behavior, he becomes visible again, things go back to normal. You give attention. You talk to him. You act as though nothing happened. It's like time stood still. Of course, he doesn't get what he wanted.

Extinguishing serves two purposes. One, it can modify your child's behavior. With no reinforcement of any kind, the kid will eventually stop the behavior. Second, it prevents you from doing or saying anything you'll regret. If you respond to the kid's annoying mode, it's easy to overreact. To blow up. To say things that hurt your child.

Banish the Bedtime Blues

Bedtime with small children can be one of the most frustrating times of the day. It is a very difficult area for many parents, so don't feel too bad. You've got a lot of company. I see many couples and single parents who allow their evenings to be ruined by a kid who won't go to bed. You need to succeed in this area because you need a break. You need several hours for yourself and your marriage. "My day with you is over" are words you must say and enforce.

I've got good news. Unless your child has some specific sleep disorder, you can get the job done. You can end a kid's day and have some time for your life. You don't have much of a life when you have kids, but you're entitled to something. The bottom line is this: Get tough and stop reinforcing the anti-bedtime behavior.

One parent is usually the wimp. That's the parent the kid targets.

I'm talking to you wimps. Stop rocking the child. Stop singing, even if you have the voice of a diva. Stop lying down in bed with the kid. Stop running to the child when he cries for you. You are reinforcing the behavior of not going to sleep. You'd cry too if you could get Mommy and Daddy to come in and coddle you.

Such elaborate and lengthy bedtime behaviors don't work. When you eventually leave, the kid still screams her head off. Your kid has to learn how to put herself to sleep. It's a basic life skill. Do you want to still be doing it for her when she's seventeen? Thirty-five?

If you're married, work together. Especially when you're beginning this new program, do it as a team. A show of unity and force lets the kid know you mean business. If you're single, don't worry. You can still do the job.

Establish the same bedtime every night. Consistency helps. Use the same routine in the half hour leading up to bedtime. We have our last drink, we read a story, we brush our little toofies, we put on our pj's, etc. No snacks or drinks just before bed. We don't want a sugar rush. We don't want more energy. We don't want them to pee (or worse), do we? We don't want their little bladders full, do we? No, we don't.

Eliminate rowdy games and wild roughhousing just before bed. Dads are usually the guilty ones here. Put the child in the room and in bed. You can spend a few minutes (five to ten, maximum) to talk, to unwind, to tuck in, and to pray. Then, you leave . . . and you stay gone. If he cries, let him cry. Crying won't hurt him. It's good for him. It cleans out his lungs. It helps tire him out so he can sleep. Crying is a beautiful thing.

Be prepared for some serious crying. Oh, the pitiful cries you're going to hear! There's nothing quite like the wretched wailing of the truly desperate child. Turn on the television or radio to block the sounds. Let at least twenty minutes go by before you go to the child, briefly, and say one comforting but firm sentence ("Suck it up, Sammy"). Then leave again. If you're married, go together.

CONSEQUENCES FOR YOUNGER KIDS

The secret is to act like you don't care. You pretend it's not fazing you. This tough exterior will crush his hopes of sucking you in. Your child may say, accusingly, "You don't even care!" Your response, with a hint of a smile is, "You're right. I don't. I stopped caring twenty minutes ago."

Go into Lockdown

If your kid has the gall to leave his room, lock him in. I will never forget the night when Sandy came up with the idea to lock our four loud, rambunctious, we-don't-want-to-go-to-bed kids in their rooms.

The blonde looked at me and said, "Dave, I can reverse the locks and lock them in their rooms." After a moment of stunned silence, I said in a loud voice, "I married a genius!"

Kids absolutely hate to be locked in. They love the hall light. They worship the hall light. It's like a god to them. "I have to be able to see the hall light!"

Your position is, "If you stay in bed and stay quiet, I'll leave your door open and you can see the hall light. You can stare at it all night and burn your retinas out. But if you make noise or leave your room, I'll lock you in."

On the nights when one of our little Clarkes chose to break these bedtime rules, she had her door locked. We left a night-light on, then when we went to bed we'd open her door. She'd be asleep, right by the door, her little hands reaching out for the hall light. Pathetic. We'd put her in bed and leave her door open.

If the kid cries during the night, after you're in bed, it's the same drill. Go and deal with him briefly (together, if you're married), then leave. If he comes to your bed, quickly escort him back to his bed. Do not let a child sleep in your bed, unless he's sick or genuinely terrified of something. Even in that case, it's better to take him to his bed and lie down with him.

The message is: You sleep in your bed, not mine (or ours). If you allow the child to sleep in your bed, you'll be stuck with the world's biggest fidget. Most kids thrash around in their sleep. Plus, and this is the critical part, you will establish a pattern. He'll like it in your bed and keep coming. You need your undisturbed sleep. You and your spouse need the time alone. And then, there's your child's full bladder to think of . . .

These action steps will keep your younger children in line. Now, I'll explain my consequences for older children.

YOUR BATTLE PLAN

1. Were you spanked as a child? If so, what impact did it have on you?

2. Do you have a problem with spanking your children? If so, why?

3. What will be difficult about doing time-out for your kids?

4. What kind of bedtime issues do you have with your kids? What are you doing that is encouraging the behavior of not going to bed?

5. Are you willing to try the idea of locking your kid's door at night? What would stop you from doing this?

6. Do you allow your children to sleep in your bed? Why? Are you ready to stop allowing this?

CHAPTER 17

CONSEQUENCES FOR OLDER KIDS

WHEN CHILDREN HIT eleven years of age, they go through an amazing transformation. It's a drastic, dramatic change that turns a family upside down. Suddenly, and without warning, eleven-year-old children become brilliant. Overnight, they gain wisdom and insight beyond their years. They go to bed regular kids and wake up Albert Einsteins. They know how the world works. They have a firm command of the truth in every field of study. They understand the mysteries of life. They speak with authority on issues they haven't studied.

Eleven-year-olds don't have to study and gain knowledge with time and hard work. That process is only for run-of-the-mill, average drones. Eleven-year-olds can build a mountain of theory from one tiny shred of information they overheard in the school hallway. They don't have to research the topic. What a waste of time that would be! They just know. They just know everything.

Their arguments are often ridiculous and make no sense at all, but they expect the Nobel Prize for their insights. If we try to correct them and point out the flaw in their reasoning, they shake their heads sadly in amusement. They pity us because our aging brains can no longer keep up with them. You see, as their brains expand and swell, our brains contract and shrivel. The eleven-year-olds of this world really believe parents are a bunch of doddering old fools who don't have a clue. We can't possibly match their superior intellectual prowess.

And unfortunately for us parents, this phenomenon just gets worse in the years to come. The older kids get, the smarter they think they are, and the dumber they think we are. They think we're idiots! They can't believe we've lived so long and yet know so little. To them, parents are outdated relics of the past who can't hope to outwit them. Ah, the arrogance of youth!

What our kids don't realize is that we're not as dumb as they think we are. We are getting older and somewhat creakier, but we haven't lost it yet. As a matter of fact, we know more than they do. A lot more. We can outsmart them. We can stay one jump ahead of them. We can teach them what they must know about life without them even knowing we're doing it.

One of the ways we teach life skills is through consequences. We will, over and over again, correct bad behavior by hitting them where it hurts. Through the pain of consequences will come critical tools for living a successful life.

If They Like It, You Can Use It

You can use anything older kids value for punishment. When I say anything, I mean anything. The list goes on and on: smartphone and all electronic devices, car, money, job, fun food, any sport or activity, social life and dating, television, video games, bicycle, skateboard, bedtime, music, crossword puzzles . . .

All kids have certain things they like. That's what you take—piece by little piece.

The first seven on my list are what I call the "biggies." In my experience, these seven items are highly valued by older kids and so can be used very effectively as consequences.

Smartphone

This is the Big Kahuna of valued items. Your kid's phone, as you well know, is his whole stinking life! Your phone is probably your whole stinking life, too, but that's another story. Your kid's phone is his connection to friends, social life, social media, entertainment (all the little videos he watches), music, cultural news, sports highlights and updates, games, traffic reports, GPS . . .

He can't stand being out of the loop and cut off from his entire world. He simply cannot live without his phone. But he'll have to—at least for a while—if he chooses to disobey your rules.

When you take his phone (or her phone), he'll whine: "But, what if I'm having an emergency?" The only emergency is he doesn't have his phone. Tell him, with a straight face, "All your friends have phones. At least, the ones who follow their parents' rules. Use one of their phones."

I include in this smartphone category every other electronic device. During the period of punishment, I would allow use of a computer for homework. Homework is its own punishment.

Car

The bad news is your kid is driving and that's terrifying. Not to mention what you're paying in insurance—that's the really terrifying part. But the good news is you can take your kid's driver's license and she can't drive. It's a beautiful thing. Not being able to drive stings like a whip.

Part of this no car consequence is you driving your kid to school. For a teenager, there's not much worse than being dropped off at school by your mommy. This can be pretty entertaining for you. Parental payback is sweet!

Drive right up to the school's main entrance with your windows down and loud Christian music playing. The old hymns of the faith, preferably. As you try to hug your kid, say in a loud voice, "Give Mommy a kiss, sweetie! Mommy loves you!"

Money

Cash is king. Your kid loves money because it buys him things he wants. He'll hate having some of his own money taken away. So take it away. This is a powerful consequence.

If you want to have some real fun, set up a mock courtroom in your living room. As the judge, wear a powdered wig and levy fines. This will create changed behavior and give you more money. So you can buy things *you* want.

Job

If your kid has a job, he obviously values it and the money it provides. Since he's living in your home, you will decide—based on his behavior—whether he keeps the job. If he continues to break your rules, you will talk to his boss and the job will go away. He'll have to earn the right to get another job.

Fun Food

Withholding junk food, snacks, and dessert are excellent consequences. "Hey, where are the Twinkies, the Pepsi, and the potato chips?" "They're gone, Bobby. Because of your behavior, there will be no snacks for three days. But help yourself to the cauliflower and carrot sticks."

Keep feeding your kid the basic meals, of course: "Here are your vegetables. Eat up, honey." The nice thing about this consequence is there are more snacks available for you!

Any Sport or Activity

School activities and sports are fair game. So are outside-of-school activities: a community-based sport, martial arts, dance, music, Boy Scouts, Girl Scouts . . . You take away the sport or the activity. She misses a practice or a game.

Some parents tell me, "But that hurts the whole team!" I say, "Yes, it does. And whose fault is that?" The parents mumble, "Well, I guess it's Susie's fault." I reply, "Yeah, I guess it is."

Always have your kid call the coach or the adult leader of the activity and explain why she can't be there. This is part of the consequence. Listen in so her explanation is accurate, and that she is actually talking to the person.

She might get a little inventive: "Coach, my mom's a real witch! I think she's bipolar!"

And you say to your child, "If baseball (or basketball or dance or music lessons or fill in the blank) is important to you, I guess you'll follow the rules."

Social Life and Dating

If you want to cause pain and anguish (and change behavior), limit your kid's social life. Going to a friend's house, having a friend over to your house, hanging out at the mall or the park, and attending parties are all on the table.

Dating can also be suspended. Dating is not a right. It's not mentioned in the United States Constitution. I checked. "You will not talk on the phone or go out with Bobby for one week."

Your daughter will whine, "I can't live without Bobby!" You

respond, "Then I guess we'll plan a funeral, because you ain't seeing him." And you'll add, "If Bobby means so much to you, then I guess you'll follow the rules. You never have to miss a moment with that punk . . . I mean, that fine young man."

When you apply one of these consequences, your kid will often try that universally cherished statement of teenage angst: "But that's not fair!" You reply, stone-faced: "Our having to raise you . . . *that's* not fair."

These consequences for older kids will be effective. But I'm not done yet. I want you to have every possible consequence in your repertoire, so there are some more in the next chapter.

YOUR BATTLE PLAN

1. Talk about what each of your children values. What is most important to each of them? Are you willing to use what they value as consequences?

2. Of my seven "biggies," which ones do your kids value the most? Have you used any of these "biggies" yet to punish?

3. Of these seven "biggies," which ones will be the hardest for you to use as consequences? Why will these be so hard to use?

CHAPTER 18

MORE CONSEQUENCES FOR OLDER KIDS

ONCE CHILDREN MOVE into elementary school, they have a mind—and a mouth—of their own. They also have a will—in some cases, a strong will. Fortunately for you, they also have a life filled with things they enjoy. All the things they enjoy are ammunition for your discipline strategy.

As my favorite World War II warrior, General George S. Patton, used to say: "Hit 'em where it hurts, boys!"

Again, just to be clear, you create pain for your kids not out of anger or revenge, but for their own good. The consequences in my system are designed to save your kid's lives, teach them essential life skills, and shape them into godly persons.

A Daily System

Every time the sun comes up, it's a new day and the slate is clean. Your child has a golden opportunity to avoid consequences and earn rewards. If your child makes good choices, he chooses to have a good day. If he makes poor choices, he chooses to have a bad day.

The kind of day he has is entirely up to him. You don't care either way, and you make this lack of caring clear to him: "My day won't be affected by how you choose to behave, but your day will."

In the morning, your child gets up on time and does the few chores required of him. He gets dressed and has an on-time departure from your home to school. So far, so good. He's on track to have a good day and earn the privilege to do the fun things he enjoys later in the day.

After school, he gets his homework done without you having to nag him. He did not have any academic or behavioral issues at his school. He completes his assigned chores.

Now, he has earned an enjoyable rest of the day. He can do what he wants to do: go outside, watch television, use his phone to text friends and play games and watch videos, go to a game or a practice, go to music or dance or martial arts, go to bed at his usual time . . .

If, however, he chooses to get out of bed late and fails to do his morning chores, there will be a reduction in his after-school fun activities. For example, his phone time could be limited to twenty minutes and he cannot watch television.

After school, he fights you on his homework and does a lousy job on his chores. His penalty for these poor choices is no phone time the rest of the day, no time outside, and an earlier bedtime.

If his behavior is particularly obnoxious and defiant, he will lose *all* his typical privileges for the day. He won't be going outside, he won't have his phone, he won't watch television, he won't go to any activity or sport, he won't get dessert or snacks, and he'll go to bed early. Basically, grounded for the day.

And *no one cares*. You, the parent, not caring that he is mad and upset, may be his worst punishment. A miserable kid wants you to be miserable too. This is his way of punishing you. When you smile and laugh and carry on as if nothing has happened, he suffers alone. That's a good thing.

No matter what has happened the previous day, when morning comes he has a brand-new chance to choose to follow the rules. It's a fresh start and he can earn all the privileges he desires today.

My daily system has proven effective for most kids, including the strong-willed variety. Tough, difficult kids act out a lot, so it's easy to pile on consequences that last days or weeks. They could end up grounded for months!

With my system, these kids have a new opportunity every day to make better choices and earn what they want. If they continue to act out every day, they will choose to be grounded every day. Eventually, they'll realize they are the only ones suffering and they'll improve their behavior.

Make Consequences Specific and Time-Limited

Consequences need to be specific so they're clear. They need to be time-limited to provide consistency and hope. Don't say, "You're grounded for life!" It's kind of impossible to enforce this consequence. "I'm twenty-four now, Dad. Can I go out now?" "No, I said for life, Bobby!"

It's better to clearly define the grounding. "You are grounded for one week, beginning tonight and going through next Monday night. Grounded means no use of your phone or any electronic device, no dates, no friends over, no visits to friends' houses, and no use of the car except to and from school. Each violation of the grounding rules will add one day to the grounding." Theoretically, it could be for life, but that's unlikely. Have the kid repeat the consequences so you can know she has it. Close all the loopholes. All kids are born lawyers.

For major violations (poor grades due to laziness, extreme disrespect, lying, stealing, outright defiance, alcohol or drug use, sexting, etc.), your consequences will be more severe, last longer, and remain in place until real change occurs.

I had a case where an eighteen-year-old boy showed disrespect for his dad big-time in front of the entire family. I recommended the dad lower the boom. The boy's car was taken away for a minimum of two weeks. He had to apologize to the entire family—and mean it. He had to show real, measurable change in a number of areas before the car was returned. There was an evaluation at the end of each week. As I recall, it took that boy four weeks to get his car back.

Don't Nag, Just Get Even

At most, ask your child only one time to do something. Tell her exactly what you want done, and give a time frame: right now, within ten minutes, by 5:00 p.m. If the job isn't done correctly or within the time frame, lay a consequence on the kid. She'll still do the job, but then suffer the consequence. This approach will save you a lot of time, energy, and stress. It will also improve your relationship with your child.

When you keep reminding a kid to do something, you are a nag. You get angrier and angrier, don't you? Finally, you lose it. "Cindy, I've told you to pick up your clothes five times! Pick them up, now!" Actually, it's your own mistake for telling her five times. That's four times too many. When you lose it, it's your fault in the kid's mind. You are the issue, not the fact that she stalled and disobeyed and didn't do what you asked, when you asked.

Your kid wants you to lose it. She feels powerful: "Look what I did to Mom. She's freaking out!" A really difficult, strong-willed kid loves to get a reaction out of you. And this kind of kid is good at it. Your reaction is her payoff. She doesn't even care if you punish her. She got what she wanted. She got you mad.

When your child disobeys, you have to act as though you don't care. You have to take all the emotion out of the situation. What the kid did means nothing to you. She acted out or didn't do that chore—so what? You don't care. You point it out in an even, calm tone, and lay the consequences on her. "You made a poor choice, and here's the consequence." No anger. No hurt. No nagging. No emotional outbursts. No lectures.

If you can reduce the emotion and just hit the kid with the consequence, some nice things happen. First, you'll be in control, and you'll maintain your dignity and respect. When you lose it, you really do look stupid: distorted facial features like bulging eyes, swelling neck veins, and flecks of foam spraying from your mouth. Second, there's no payoff for the kid. There's no attention and no power. Just the consequence. Maybe—just maybe—the kid will walk away blaming herself. Third, you don't waste your precious time nagging, blowing up, and then having to apologize. The kid makes a mistake, you lower the boom with surgical precision, and life moves on. My mother has a saying: "The little dogs bark, but the caravan moves on."

I'm not quite done with consequences for older children. Next, I cover four more tried-and-true discipline strategies.

YOUR BATTLE PLAN

1. Does my daily system make sense to you? What will cause you trouble in following it?

2. How good are you at "not caring" when your children act out? What do they do or say that gets you visibly upset?

3. Are you guilty of not being clear when you ground your child? What will be hard about being specific when you use grounding?

4. How many times, on average, do you have to ask each of your children to do something? (If you're not sure, ask them . . . they'll know.)

5. What happens when you nag and then lose your temper? How does the child respond? How do you feel afterward?

CHAPTER 19

EVEN MORE CONSEQUENCES
FOR OLDER KIDS

KIDS ARE SMART. They're clever. They want their way, and they'll do whatever it takes to get their way. Often, their way is not good for them.

The geniuses who believe kids were born without a sin nature don't have kids.

You have to be smarter. You have to be cleverer. (Is that a word?) You need to utilize strategic consequences to guide your kids the right way. God's way.

Here are my four final consequences for older kids.

Creative Consequences

Be creative with some of your consequences. Come up with crazy, zany ideas for correcting your kids. The element of humor eases the blow and can help motivate change. This approach keeps your kids guessing and makes parenting more fun for you.

For example, I saw a mom in therapy who came up with an ingenious way to get her kids up in the morning. She was having fits dragging them out of bed in time to leave for school. They were chronically late and ruined her mornings. She decided to take action.

Her plan was to give them one wake-up call at 6:45 a.m. If they weren't up by 7:00, she'd walk in and soak them with a pitcher of ice water—right in the kisser. She told me that after a few soakings they became early risers. The kids could hear the ice machine, and then the splashing of the water in the pitcher as Mom came down the hallway. You never saw kids leap so fast out of bed.

Another mom used funny, silly behaviors as consequences for her son. Her behavior wasn't mean, just tongue-in-cheek. Her method was to make him do more of the unacceptable, impulsive, immature actions he engaged in at home.

If he ran into the house, she'd say, "Okay, everybody outside and let's watch Jimmy (not his real name) run." The whole family, and neighborhood kids too, if they were present, would troop outside. She had Jimmy run laps and wind sprints.

If Jimmy (who was an aggressive child) pushed someone else, she'd say, "I guess you like to push. So let's do some pushing." She'd make him push the wall for a few minutes. There was a time when Jimmy had a bad habit of spitting. That's right—you guessed it—when she caught him spitting, she'd say, "I guess you like to spit. Here's a bucket. Fill it up."

Natural Consequences

Natural consequences are the consequences that naturally occur following a behavior. It's simply allowing nature to run its course. You, the parent, do nothing. God is the One who came up with the idea of natural consequences: "Whatever one sows, that will he also reap" (Galatians 6:7).

If your kid works hard in school, he will get good grades. If he goofs off, he'll get poor grades. If your daughter breaks driving laws, she'll get a ticket or may end up in an accident. If your son lies to his friends, they won't trust him.

Don't step in to save your child from natural consequences. There are some lessons that only life can teach. I know parents who have marched in to complain to a teacher about a low grade. The kid earned the low grade, but Mommy and Daddy tried to get it raised.

Once I saw a couple in therapy whose son got busted for dealing drugs. They admitted to me that he was guilty of the crime. I told these Christian parents to have their son plead guilty and throw himself on the mercy of the court. They disagreed, and ended up mortgaging their home to pay for an expensive attorney. Their son pled not guilty! It was disgraceful. This entitled young man, who should have paid for his crime, beat the rap! Guess what happened one year later? You know what happened. He was arrested again for dealing drugs. What a shocker.

You intervene only in a situation when serious physical harm or injustice will take place. If your child's life is at risk, you'll do whatever it takes to save her. If others are lying, and your kid is being blamed for something he didn't do, you will take action.

But if your kid makes a poor choice, let life's natural consequences follow.

Logical Consequences

Logical consequences are the consequences you as the parent apply. There are many times, such as with poor grades, when you will apply logical consequences on top of natural consequences. Try to make sure the consequences are logically related to the misbehavior. If you can connect the two logically, the consequence has more punch and

PARENTING IS HARD AND THEN YOU DIE

will be remembered. There's a better chance change will be created. In other words, the punishment should fit the crime.

Here's an example of a wrong approach: Your child fails to take out the trash, and you ground him for one week. Where's the logical connection? Here's a better way: The kid fails to take out the trash, and you make him eat part of the trash. I'm kidding, of course. A logical consequence would be not paying him for that job.

Here are more examples: The kid breaks a curfew, he's grounded for one week. You see, that's logical. He was out late, so he doesn't get to go out again for a while. The kid drives poorly or misuses the car, his or her driving privileges are suspended for a period of time. The kid misuses the television; no television for a period of time. The kid abuses his phone privileges; no phone for however long you determine it will take him to learn his lesson. The kid makes a mess, she cleans it up.

The kid fails to put dirty clothes in the hamper; you don't wash them. (By the way, it's a hamper—stop calling it a laundry basket.) Your kid will complain, "But my clothes smell! I have nothing clean to wear to school." You say, "Don't worry, Son, I think most of the other kids smell too." I'll just bet you'll find your son's clothes in the hamper later on that day.

Make Misbehavior a Family Issue

The power and support of the family is often overlooked in the process of discipline. The family is the unit God designed to help us learn, grow, and adjust in life (Deuteronomy 6:5-7). Let's use it!

When a child misbehaves, at first you deal only with that child. If the child is genuinely repentant and demonstrates change, you can keep the matter confidential. The rest of the family will know generally what's going on, but you keep the details private.

But if there is no repentance and no change, take it to the family.

If your child has an unhealthy, serious behavior problem that is not improving—alcohol, drugs, sex, cheating in school, poor grades, lying, disrespect for parents and authority figures, harming another family member, breaking the law, associating with bad peers—take it to the family.

Take it to the family means you call a meeting of the immediate nuclear family. Everyone living under one roof attends the meeting. If Grandma is in the back bedroom, drag her to the meeting—well, just ask her to come. The misbehaving child is at the meeting, even if you have to hold her down.

You reveal the specific problem in detail. First, you ask the child to tell the family about the problem. If she refuses, then you do it, perhaps explaining that it might be fairer and more accurate if she explained things in her own words. You go over all of it, chapter and verse. The consequence of the whole family knowing carries some weight. Even a hard-nosed kid will feel the heat. Since one member's behavior affects the whole family, the family has a right to know. Plus, a family is supposed to be a group whose members love each other and care about one another.

In this initial meeting, the parent in charge asks each member to comment on the situation. You go around the room and, one by one, everyone shares, following just a few simple rules (for example, no insults allowed, no self-righteousness). Family members can express anger, hurt, and disappointment. Members can admit how they've contributed to the problem. Plans and strategies for solving the problem can be discussed. Members can share how they handled a similar problem in their lives.

The support, feedback, and advice of the family is invaluable in solving the problem. It's the family working together to help one of its own. It's not an individual problem. It's a family problem. The family members don't trash the misbehaving child; they try to help. When one family member hurts, everybody hurts. As in the church, when one member rejoices, the others rejoice with her; when one member suffers, the others suffer too (1 Corinthians 12:26).

What I am suggesting is similar to what I do as a psychologist in family therapy. I bring the whole family together in my office. I never know who will be the key to change. Sometimes it's the youngest member. Sometimes it's the oldest. Time and time again I've seen God use family meetings to create real healing and change.

At the end of this meeting, the family prays for the child who is acting out and for the family. Each member offers a prayer. It's vital to involve God and ask for His help. Jesus gave us two wonderful promises in Matthew 18:19-20: "Again I say to you, if two of you agree on earth about anything they ask, it will be done for them by my Father in heaven. For where two or three are gathered in my name, there am I among them."

No problem is ever solved without God.

Have regular family meetings to check on the child's progress and to hold her accountable. You can use your regular once-a-week family meeting to deal with this ongoing situation. Difficult problems take time to fix, so a number of meetings may be necessary. Meet for as many weeks as it takes to achieve a breakthrough. After all, a member of the family is worth the trouble.

You might want to try a technique I often use with my families in therapy. I ask the parents to each write a letter to the misbehaving child. The letter consists of two parts. One, all the resentments they feel for the child. Two, what they admit is their responsibility for the problem. They confess their personal failings and shortcomings as parents.

I ask the child to write the same letter, which describes her resentment against her parents and her responsibility in creating and maintaining the problem.

Then I have all three read their letters out loud in front of the entire family in a session. It's powerful, and it can be very healing. I make it clear when I give the assignment that it has three goals: to get all the issues out on the table, to begin to clean out all resentments and promote forgiveness, and to begin a process of change. After the letters are read, they are burned with the whole family watching.

In certain situations, it's a good idea to add others outside the nuclear family to your meetings: extended family, close family friends, teachers, coaches, pastors, etc. If the one-on-one approach doesn't work, you go to the nuclear family meetings. If the nuclear family meetings don't work, call in more troops. You may have to end up renting a gymnasium.

Matthew 18:15-17 teaches us this very principle. When someone is in sin, go to him individually. If he doesn't listen, go to him with two or three others. If he still won't listen, go to the church body with the problem. So if your child doesn't respond, keep adding more persons to the process.

Okay, that's it for consequences. These consequences will work to shape your child into a responsible and godly person, but only if you add rewards to your discipline operation.

YOUR BATTLE PLAN

1. Did your parents use creative, out-of-the-box consequences with you? If so, what did they do and did it work?

2. Have you used creative consequences with your kids? If so, what did you do and did it work?

3. When you were growing up, what natural consequences did you suffer? Did these consequences change your behavior?

4. Do you allow natural consequences to impact your kids? If not, why not?

5. Did your parents use logical consequences with you? If so, what were they and did they work?

6. Do you use logical consequences with your kids? If not, why not? What are two logical consequences you can use right now with your children?

7. What would stop you from making misbehavior a family issue? Are you willing to use the family as a tool of discipline?

CHAPTER 20

REWARDS MUST BE EARNED

I HAVE ONLY one chapter on rewards. Rewards are a key part of my system of discipline, but they are a lot easier to apply than consequences. When rewards are given out, everyone is happy and life is good.

Nightmare on Main Street

Back when our three girls were small, the five of us (William wasn't around yet) drove to Orlando to spend the day at Disney World. We hadn't been there for a while, and Sandy and I thought the kids would really enjoy it. As I paid several hundred dollars for our entrance tickets, it began to dawn on me why we hadn't been there for a while. That day was the longest day of my life. It still gives me the willies to think about it.

It was hot. Brutally hot. The heat was not just from the sun. It was body heat coming from the unbelievable mass of humanity clogging every square foot of the Magic Kingdom. We waited in interminable lines for everything. We waited to see Mickey and Minnie. We waited to get a drink of water. We waited for the little train that chugs around the park. We waited to order lunch. We waited until a table opened up for lunch. (I had to yell, "Fire!" to clear some space.) We waited to throw out our trash from lunch. We waited to go to the bathroom. But most of all, we waited in line for the rides. Hours and hours of waiting for rides, each of which lasted a couple of minutes.

My breaking point came at the Dumbo ride late in the afternoon. Leeann just had to go on Dumbo, so we joined the back of the line. You couldn't even see the ride from where we were. I really thought I was going to die in that line. Several folks ahead of us did collapse from heatstroke, and I silently cheered when their absence moved the line a few yards. Hey, it was survival of the fittest.

After an hour and a half, we finally got there and climbed into the flying Dumbo vehicle. We rose up and flew in a circle for a lousy, crummy, and insulting ninety seconds. As Dumbo returned to earth, I told Leeann to stay put. When the uniformed attendant came up to ask us to get out, I said through clenched teeth, "I waited an hour and a half for this pitiful ninety seconds. We're going around again." I think that scene cost us the chance to be the featured family in the next Main Street Parade. I didn't actually have the nerve to stay on the ride. I realized I would have been torn to bits by the poor suckers still waiting for their ninety-second ride.

Leeann and I left the scene of the Dumbo nightmare and met up with Sandy and the other two girls at a predetermined spot. One look at Sandy and I knew her day had been even worse than mine. Nancy had thrown up all over the front of Mom's blouse. Not spit up. Thrown up. Upchucked. You could smell her thirty yards away. That was the second thing that disqualified us from being the Parade family.

Sandy told me later that a lady had asked her, "Did you know that your child threw up all over you?" Sandy told her, "No! Really? Is that what this awful smelling stuff is all over my blouse?" There were two good results from Nancy's little accident. One, it certainly cleared a path through the crowd. Two, it brought our day to an end. Sandy said to me, "We're going home." I didn't argue.

The five of us came dragging down Main Street. Sandy and I were exhausted and in extremely foul moods. If Goofy had gotten in my way, I would have flattened him. It should have been obvious to everyone that we needed to go home.

But what did my two older daughters do? Did Emily and Leeann thank us for the day? Did they sympathize with our ragged, limp-as-a-noodle condition? Did they at least have the common courtesy to be quiet? No! They cried and whined and begged to go on just a few more rides. They told us we couldn't leave Disney World early! They said we just had to stay for them. They wanted more fun and we owed it to them. If you want to know what happened when we got back home, read my section on spanking in chapter 16.

This story doesn't surprise you, does it? I'm sure you could tell many stories just like it. All kids believe that their parents owe them a very nice living. They take and take and take and come back for more. They have an inborn, ingrained entitlement attitude.

Kids also believe they shouldn't have to do anything in return for all the wonderful pleasures afforded them in life. They fully expect their parents to grant their every whim just because these darlings are alive. Their motto is: "We didn't ask to be born. But now that we're here, you've got to give us what we want."

Everything Is a Reward

Part of good parenting is correcting this entitlement attitude. In fact, there are only a few physical things kids are entitled to: food, water, shelter, clothing, and medical care. That's it. Everything—and I mean everything—else is a luxury item and, therefore, a reward. Rewards are the same things you take away to create consequences. It's the same list I used in chapter 17. Basically, rewards are anything your kids value. You put the whole enchilada, whatever they like, on the table.

The trick is to find out what each kid values. Then, you can use the rewards to motivate. Some parents ask me, "Why do you have to use rewards? Shouldn't kids do things because those things are right? Surely you're not telling me we should reward children for being good?"

My reply is, "Get real. Join me in the real world!" You have to motivate kids. Eventually, they'll internalize and do good things because it makes them feel good inside, and because it will please God. But this process takes time! God uses rewards. He always has. When we obey His standards, He rewards us. Don't forget, there will be rewards in heaven (Luke 6:23).

Cut a Deal

Ask your kid what he wants in return for a behavior you want him to do. Cut a deal! If he's an older kid, does he want money, television time, phone time, computer time, or a later bedtime? If he's a younger kid, does he want a special video, to play with a special toy, to play outside, or a coloring book or stickers?

Sandy's potty training method was simple and effective—and based on rewards. If the child went to the pot, she got a chocolate treat. If she wet her pants, she got nothing. And she had to clean up her mess. That was the consequence part. Wiping up a yellow river, or picking up a Number Two and putting it in the pot was not pleasant. Of course, we didn't make the kids use their bare hands.

Let's say you want to motivate your child to read. If you're like

Sandy and me, you consider reading of the utmost importance. You need to model reading. You need to read often to your child. You need to find enjoyable books for him to read. And you need to cut a deal!

In return for twenty minutes a day of reading, what does he want? It's not enough to say, "You know, Billy, reading is very important. So we'd like you to read more. Okay?" Initially, you motivate him to read with rewards. When he eventually enjoys reading, his own enjoyment will be his reward.

Make Your Child Earn Rewards

All kids think the things they value are God-given rights, and they shouldn't have to do anything in return for them. Wrong! Your kids must earn rewards and keep on earning them. "The last time I checked, Bobby, you weren't part of the royal family. No, we're just common people, and we all have to work for what we get."

If you just hand out rewards regardless of children's behavior, you spoil them! They have no incentive to improve their behavior. You feed the entitlement attitude they already have by nature. You've got to teach your children that, in life, rewards are earned by hard work. It's true, they could eventually go on welfare and be supported by the government. But that won't be much of a life.

I worked with a dad whose teenage son had gotten hooked on drugs. He and his wife paid for several treatment programs, but the kid always went back to using. The dad came up with a plan he was sure would work. He decided to give his son a brand-new car. He told the boy, "If you stop using drugs and complete college, you can keep it."

I told the dad he was crazy! This kid didn't deserve even a go-cart! The dad meant well, but his plan was a complete disaster. His son kept using drugs. You need to make a kid earn what he gets. If you give the reward first, you take away the motivation.

Business Before Pleasure

Whenever a child wants a reward, you ask, "What are you going to do to earn it?" If your son wants to watch a video, he will first put away his toys and help Mom dust. If your daughter wants to use the phone, she will have to first finish her homework and chores. If he wants to go outside and play, he will get his chores done. If she wants dessert, she will eat a good dinner and help clean up after dinner. Now, you don't always do this. But almost always. Business before pleasure is a life principle kids need to learn before they leave your home.

Let's say your teen wants a bigger reward: driving a car, going on a date, having you pay car insurance, having you pay for a phone, or having a later curfew. These are bigger privileges, and your child will have to produce bigger behavior to get them: grades high, chores done, behavior good, church attendance solid, and spiritual life strong.

I think you've got the picture. Everything is earned. My dad told me over and over, "David, if you decide to live a lifestyle we don't approve of—drinking, drugs, sex, drifting from God—then we will not subsidize your lifestyle. We will not pay for private high school. We won't pay one thin dime for college. And you won't live here."

This message helped keep me on the straight and narrow. To my parents, three things would determine whether or not my brother and I would receive rewards (including use of the car): our relationship with the Lord, our behavior, and our grades. This was a straight "reward/consequence" strategy.

Rewards Given Can Be Taken Away

Just because children have earned a reward doesn't mean they get to keep it. It all depends on their behavior. Kids think that once they earn a reward it's theirs, even if they blow it big time behavior-wise. I say no. You can take back a reward if necessary.

Jimmy earns the right to watch a favorite video. Just before he watches it, he starts a fight with his sister and slaps her across the face. What do you do? Easy. You yank the video, and you add some other consequences. He'll say, "But I earned that video!" You will say, "That's right, son, you did. But you just 'de-earned' it. But don't worry, you can earn it again, after you've paid this debt to society."

Susie earned your permission to go to her first formal banquet at school. It's a big deal! She has her dress, her date, and all the plans are in place. Susie's report card comes in a few days before the banquet and it's a disaster: two F's, two D's, and one C. What do you do?

You cancel the banquet. She knew she was doing poorly, and she said nothing to you. Some parents would say, "Oh, but what about her date? The poor guy's not going to be able to go now." Here's what I say to the young man: "Timmy, you rolled the dice when you asked my daughter out. You gambled, son. And in this case, you lost! It's over. Next time, ask a girl who has better grades."

Losing the banquet is a bitter pill for Susie, but it'll be a consequence she'll never forget. "The parent giveth, and the parent taketh away" (Hezekiah 22:12). Okay, this verse isn't in the Bible. But the principle certainly is—all through both Testaments. Love is unconditional, but material gifts and rewards are not.

Even if a kid has bought something with his own money, you can take it away. The kid is living in your home, isn't he? Sometimes you have to give your kid this message: "Me parent. You child. Me take."

A single mom spoke to me at a parenting seminar I was presenting at her church. Her seventeen-year-old son had made a big mistake and she asked what consequences would be appropriate. I recommended, among other things, that she take away his car for a while. She said, "I can't do that. He bought his own car and he's paying his own car insurance." I said, "That doesn't make any difference. He lives in your home, doesn't he? You're the mom, aren't you? Take the car."

Cash Money Motivates

Go ahead and use money as a reward. It isn't the only reward you use, but it can be a powerful one. Use money in return for household chores. Pay a specific amount for a specific job. When it's done to your satisfaction and in your time frame, pay the kid.

This is the way life works. Do a job, get paid. Isn't money one of the main reasons you work? Now, you don't give money for every single job. "Thanks for holding the door, John. Here's a fiver." Or "I appreciate you helping carry the groceries in, Becky. Here's two dollars." I don't believe in tipping kids.

I like this system for chores: The kids are responsible for certain core chores. No money is given for these duties. They are done to help out the family to which they belong. If these regular chores aren't done, there are consequences. Then, there is also a list of extra jobs. For these, money is given. This system provides a good, realistic balance. In life, you're not paid for every job you do, especially around the home.

Money for good grades is a good idea. If it works for your kid, do it! Work out a deal: thirty dollars for every A, twenty-five dollars for a B, etc. I wouldn't pay for C's and D's. When you pay him off, your kid will walk away and think, "Ha! What a sucker!" He'll laugh to himself as he counts his cash. "This is the easiest money I ever made." Well, the joke's on him. He studied and he learned. That's all you care about.

Discipline is a very complicated, difficult, and frustrating area. On many days you'll feel just like God did about the Israelites: "I spread out my hands all the day to a rebellious people, who walk in a way that is not good" (Isaiah 65:2).

It's easy to give up and think your kids will never learn how to obey. But don't give up. Hang in there. Keep on doing the right things and in time you will be rewarded for your perseverance. You will receive the wonderful blessing promised in Proverbs 29:17: "Discipline your son, and he will give you rest; he will give delight to your heart."

In a world that has no discipline and is falling apart, with God's help we can teach our children limits. If we have no one else but God to help us, He is enough.

The behavior-based system I have described is the most effective system of discipline I've ever discovered. It has helped Sandy and me. It has helped many parents I've worked with in therapy and taught in my seminars. God has used it to make a difference in the lives of many parents and their kids. If you use it, it will help you.

It's time to tackle teenagers. Notice the neat alliteration in that last sentence? You know, all the words beginning with *t*? Anyway, people are always complaining about the terrible twos. That's a joke. It should be the terrible teens!

The teen years are very challenging years, for you and your kids. The teen years are when your kids decide who they are and how they will live their lives.

If you can understand the massive changes every teenager goes through and how to respond to those changes, you'll do a good job as a parent.

I'm going to help you do that.

YOUR BATTLE PLAN

1. Bring up a time when your kids showed their entitlement attitude. What was your response?

2. Do you believe that you have to motivate your kids with rewards? If not, why not?

3. Are you giving your children rewards without their having to earn them? If so, what is the impact on your kids?

4. Are you willing to follow the "business before pleasure" principle? What will be hard about following this principle?

5. Do you have a problem using money to motivate your children? If so, why? What is your system for chores? Do you pay your kids for certain chores?

PART FOUR

Teens

CHAPTER 21

"HELP ME WITH MY PHYSICAL CHANGES"

AFTER YEARS OF clinical experience, careful research, and observation, I have developed the definitive description of the typical teenager: The teenager is an intensely moody, irritable creature who has all the symptoms of PMS, a midlife crisis, and manic depression . . . at the same time.

The teenager eats a diet that would kill any other creature after several weeks: hamburgers, french fries, pizza, and candy are the staples. Vegetables are feared and avoided. Studies with rats have proven the toxic nature of the teenager's diet. The rats are fed the basic teen diet, and within ten to fourteen days, they're all dead. They drop like flies. In fact, the researchers report that these rats seem to want to die. They were lifting one dead rat (he was still holding a piece of pepperoni pizza in his little rat fist) out of his cage. The rat had written these words in the sawdust: "Please kill me."

The typical teenager lives in filth and disorder. The teen's room looks like the site of an explosion. *National Geographic* could do a series of documentaries on the various forms of insect life in the adolescent's room. These documentaries haven't been done because scientists cannot guarantee the safety of reporters and camerapersons.

Teenagers usually travel in packs called peer groups. A peer group is a group of young people trying desperately to be unique individuals, while dressing, talking, and acting exactly alike.

But the defining characteristic of the teenager is the attitude. The mean, rotten, nasty, and selfish attitude that's so common. They hate the world. They hate you. They hate sunshiny days, flower petals, birds singing, and everything nice. They don't see the glass as half empty. They see the glass as empty, with a bad stain on it, and crushed into a thousand fragments. They are "cool." You, the parent, are a nerd. They are smart; you are an idiot. They know it all; you know nothing.

My point is, the teenager is a very complicated and confusing individual. Dr. Earl Wilson, one of my professors in graduate school, defines a teenager this way: "an adult trying to happen." The main purpose of adolescence is to grow from a dependent, irresponsible child into an independent, responsible adult. This is one of the most difficult transitions in all of life.

Some teenagers seem to just sail through this time period with a minimum of stress and suffering. Notice, I said some. As in, rare. I wouldn't count on having this kind of teenager. If you're lucky enough to have one like this, you ain't gonna have two! The vast majority of teenagers find these years painful and turbulent. And, of course, so do their parents.

The Big Six

Your teenager has to become an independent, responsible adult and create an identity—all while undergoing tremendous changes in six areas:

- physical
- sexual
- emotional
- intellectual
- spiritual
- social

I call these the Big Six. And believe me, they are big. Have you ever seen one of those old horror movies where the main character is transformed from a normal person into a hideous, grotesque monster? Well, that's nothing compared to what happens to a teenager. Unlike a horror movie on television, you can't just turn it off when it gets too sickening. You've got to live with this transforming creature for at least six years!

That's the bad news. Go ahead and scream in pain. You'll feel better. The good news is, at least it's not seven years. Just kidding. The other good news is, you can survive these years and do a great job helping your teenager grow up to be a healthy, maturing adult. What you need to know as a parent is what these changes are and how, specifically, to deal with them.

In this chapter, I'll deal with the incredible *physical changes* that occur in your teenager.

Hormones on the Loose!

The physical changes in a teenager's body are rapid and spectacular. Hormones are literally running wild and producing tremendous changes in general physical development. The growth spurt occurs, making them taller and heavier. The girls usually shoot up first, which makes it tough for the boys. But most of the guys won't be midgets for long. They'll catch up and pass most of the girls a few years later. The boys' voices change, and facial and pubic hair sprouts.

Acne can be a problem for them—just when they are so conscious of their appearance!

Hormones trigger changes in sexual development. Girls begin their periods. Boys' and girls' genitals develop and mature. Your teenagers will be completely sexually mature well before the end of high school. But not necessarily sexually responsible. Your teens will be able to have sex and produce babies. That's a scary thought, isn't it?

There is a tremendous focus on physical appearance in the teen years. On every survey taken with groups of teens, physical appearance is their number one concern. Nothing else is even close. In fact, physical looks occupy the first ten spots on the list!

It is a fact of life that a teenager's self-esteem is dramatically affected by physical appearance. A teen's constant companion is the mirror. A teenager simply cannot walk past a mirror without looking. Studies have been done to prove it. Teens have been offered fabulous prizes—thousands of dollars, a new car, a day off from school—if they can just walk past a mirror and not look. They can't do it!

Help Them Feel Understood

What can you do in response to these phenomenal physical changes? I have some ideas that will help you and your teenager. First, help them feel understood. Don't try to convince them that looks aren't important. It's a waste of time, and they'll feel terribly misunderstood. Allow your teenagers to spend an hour and a half getting ready to go out. As long as they aren't late or hogging the bathroom, let them take their time. It's important to them that every hair be in place.

Praise their looks regularly. Say things like: "You look good." "I like that shirt." "That's a pretty outfit." They won't acknowledge your praise. You won't hear, "Thanks, Mom, I needed that. As you know, physical appearance is very . . ." Dream on. Just keep giving the compliments, because deep down it makes a difference.

Let them wear their hair the way they want. If they want to make it the color of a rainbow and wear it all spiked up, let them do it. If they want it long and shaggy, don't stand in their way. It may be embarrassing for you, but it isn't about you. It's about them feeling confident with their looks.

Many teens try out a variety of hairstyles as they go through high school. They're working on their individuality, trying to fit in with their peer group, and focusing on looking their best. As they reach young adulthood, they'll have normal hairstyles. Really, believe me. They will.

Tattoos, Piercings, and Other Difficult Decisions

Tattoos and piercings are very common among teenagers. Since these "accessories" have more impact on the body, you need to use a more careful approach. Do not give an immediate no, especially if you've never had a tattoo or a piercing (other than in your ear). When my kids were teens, I was often tempted to say an abrupt no to this kind of request.

But a quick no is disrespectful to your teens, cuts off communication, hurts your relationship with them, and often leads to outright (or secret) rebellion in major areas.

I strongly urge you to have a dialogue with your teens about these issues.

When you receive a request for a tattoo or a piercing, say, "I'm not going to give my response now. We need to talk about it. Take a week to think and pray about what you'd like to do with your body. Come up with a list of reasons why you want to do this, and ask God how He feels about it. I [or we, if you're married] will do the same."

"Also, come prepared to describe what type of piercing you want and where it will be." Or "I need to know what tattoo image you are thinking of and where it will be." Finally, you add, "I want you to ask three persons, friends or family, how they feel now about the tattoos (or piercings) they got. One of these persons has to be a Christian."

In the week before the meeting, discuss the issue thoroughly with the other parent. If you're divorced and remarried, also discuss the issue with your new spouse. Try to build a united front. Sometimes, especially if you're divorced, you won't be able to agree. But it's worth a try.

At the first meeting, sit in a private place (if married, it will be you and your spouse) with your teenager and allow her to state her case for the tattoo or piercing (or, if you are really lucky, both). As she (it could be he, of course) speaks, listen and reflect what she is saying and feeling. Say nothing original in this meeting. Don't disagree, don't interrupt, and don't state your position and feelings. Your job as a parent is to communicate understanding of your teen's position and emotions: what she wants, why she wants it, and how she feels about it.

If you listen attentively and respect her right to her opinions and feelings, you are building a bridge of respect. You're helping her think through the issue on a deeper level. And you're motivating her to listen to you and respect what you say when it's your turn.

It's okay to ask questions in this first meeting to clarify her position and gather information. Make sure she covers all the areas you asked her to cover: her reasons, how she thinks God views this potential action, the type of tattoo or piercing and where it will be, and the input from the three persons she interviewed. If she doesn't cover all these areas, tell her to get the added information and, when ready, schedule another meeting with you.

Once she has presented her position and given you all the requested information, set up another meeting for your response. This meeting will be in two or three days. This delay shows her you are seriously considering her request and the information she has shared.

At this response meeting, you ask her to listen and understand what you're about to say. Ask her to not interrupt and to not give her response. You will then present your position and feelings concerning the tattoo or piercing: your reasons for and against the action, how you feel God views it, the potential consequences, and your feelings about it.

You will add: "If I [or we] decide to give you permission, certain things must be true in your life: Your relationship with God must be solid and growing. You must be attending church and youth group regularly. Your grades need to be B's or higher in all subjects. You have to show good, responsible behavior in and outside our home. You need to be performing your chores at home on time and without being asked. And you will pay for the tattoo [or piercing]."

If your teenager isn't meeting these standards, she'll have to meet them before she can have what she wants. The beauty of my approach is pretty apparent. If your teen actually meets these standards, she'll decide not to do the tattoo/piercing, or if she does go for it, you won't care so much because she's doing so well in these important areas of life!

The final meeting will take place in two or three days. In this meeting you will have an open dialogue in which all the parties talk through the issue. Your teen will respond to your position and give her counterarguments. All unasked questions will be asked and answered.

If you agree to the tattoo/piercing, you will clearly define the behavior standards she must meet before she can go ahead. If she's already meeting these standards and can afford the procedure, you'll tell her to go ahead and do it.

I think you can see how this process can be applied to almost every big decision your teen will be facing. When you give and require respect, when you communicate clearly, and when you involve God in the process, better decisions will be made.

Help Them Look Their Best

Listen to me, fellow parents: Buy them the clothes that are in style. Every teenage peer group has an approved dress code. If your kids don't have the peer-approved uniform, they're spotted a mile away. They don't get into the group! You don't have to like it. It's not right. It's not fair. But it's the way it is. In my day as a teen, my peer group of guys wore brown desert boots. I still wear them. I guess I never really grew up.

I saw a kid in therapy a few years back who was a bonafide nerd. This teenage guy came walking into my office wearing a plaid button-down shirt, white socks pulled up to his knees, and dress shoes with tassels. His parents (who were nerds too) told me he was having social problems. I thought to myself, "No! Really? I can't imagine why." I told that kid, "Son, you're a nerd." I didn't tell his parents they were nerds, since they were the ones paying me. The first thing I did was to get him to change his clothes.

If acne is a problem for your kids, take action. You can't stop acne, but you can fight it and reduce its severity. Complexion is critical to your teenagers. Get them to a dermatologist pronto. It's money well spent. My folks took me when I was a teenager, and I appreciated it. I didn't thank them, but I appreciated it.

Talk About Sex

Because sex is such a critically important area, I devote the entire next chapter to it. You win or lose the battle for healthy, God-honoring sexuality in the teen years. Don't wait to deal with this issue. When your kids are out of your home, it's too late.

I'll cover sex education, premarital sex, and living together. And I won't be just sharing what a Christian psychologist and dad says about these areas. First and foremost, I'll be sharing what God says.

YOUR BATTLE PLAN

1. Recall the big physical changes you went through as a teenager. Which changes were the most difficult for you and why?

2. How did your parents deal with your physical changes? What did they do right and wrong?

3. How are you doing in helping your child feel understood and supported about his/her physical appearance? What can you do better?

4. What will be hard about following my parent-teen communication process for tattoos, piercings, and other difficult issues? How do you usually handle issues like this?

5. Are you willing to buy your teen clothes that will help him/her fit in with peers? What would stop you?

CHAPTER 22

"HELP ME WITH MY SEXUAL CHANGES"

SATAN IS GOOD at what he does. He's very, very good. What he does is lead people away from God and the Bible.

When it comes to motivating your teenagers to have sex before marriage, he's brilliant. He wants as much premarital sex as possible because it damages your teens and all their relationships.

As a bonus, premarital sex weakens the institution of marriage, and Satan hates marriage with a passion.

Since the 1960s, Satan has orchestrated an incredibly successful cultural campaign to encourage and glorify sex before marriage. Twenty-four/seven he gets his message across using every possible outlet:

- the internet
- television
- streaming video services

- social media
- radio
- billboards
- magazines
- sex education in public schools

Satan has four basic messages for teenagers in the area of sex:

Message #1: Premarital sex is normal, healthy, a lot of fun, and a rite of passage.

Message #2: If you don't have premarital sex, you are a social misfit and a pathetic loser.

Message #3: Any adult who preaches abstinence before marriage is a narrow-minded, anti-fun, mean-spirited fuddy-duddy.

Message #4: Marriage is an outdated, restrictive relationship, so just live together.

You already know this truth, but I'll tell you anyway: Satan is winning. These four messages are believed by the majority of teenagers—non-Christian and Christian.

The good news is, we parents have God on our side and we still exert significant influence in the lives of our kids. So how can we combat Satan's plan and motivate our teenagers to stay sexually pure until marriage?

Here's how.

Talk About Sex

Don't wait until you give "the talk" about the birds and the bees. That will be too little and too late. If you put it off, your kids will be taught sex by our culture and their friends. I don't think you want that.

Begin early—four or five years of age—and gradually teach them more and more about sex. And please, use the correct anatomical terms. Don't say wee-wee or peeny! It's a penis. Don't say hole or opening. Say vagina. Say clitoris. Do you want your son to say in the locker room, "Yeah, that's my wee-wee!" He'll be humiliated.

From age four or five to eleven, your main focus will be teaching your children the importance and priority of the marriage relationship. They need to understand that God intends for special, personal touching to occur only between husband and wife. You will, over these years, cover basic sexual anatomy, how babies are created through the act of sexual intercourse, and that sex is not primarily for making babies—it is a very important way for Dad and Mom to express love for each other.

Up to age eleven, do your best to shield them from the world's distorted view of sex. Limit their exposure to television, the internet, and social media. You will not be entirely successful, so expect them to see and read and hear inappropriate sexual content. When this happens, encourage them to talk in detail about what they have been exposed to and how they feel and think about it. Encourage them to ask all the questions about sex they want and answer each question directly and honestly.

Teach God's view of sex at every opportunity. God's view is abstinence before marriage. Please join Sandy and me in teaching abstinence. Abstinence means no sexual activity. This is, in fact, not God's recommendation; it is God's command (1 Corinthians 6:18-20; 1 Thessalonians 4:3-4).

Do not advise your kids to use condoms or any form of birth control. I can't believe the number of Christian parents making this mistake. This is approving premarital sex and handing your teenagers a license to have sex. There is no safe sex outside of marriage—period.

Can you imagine Jesus Christ saying, "Well, I guess you're going to have sex anyway. Go ahead and sin, but just be careful." Never. I believe it is possible for teenagers to choose to refrain from engaging in sexual activity. If they have been involved, it's possible for them to stop.

Present a Comprehensive, Biblical View of Sex

What your teenagers need is a comprehensive, brutally honest, biblical view of sex. This information, delivered in the right way, will get them to critically evaluate culture's narrow, deceptive, sinful view of sex.

A book you read with your teens will not be effective. A lecture or two from you will not be effective. Your teens live in a video world, so it makes sense to use a video series to present God's view of sex.

I highly recommend *The Whole Sex Talk*. It is a multimedia, six-session program for parents and their teenagers. Each thirty-minute session is designed to assist parents to open up dialogue with their kids and help them make good choices in their sexual lives.

This video series covers every pertinent facet of sexuality. It is biblical, intensely practical, thought provoking, and entertaining. It makes a very strong case for sexual purity before marriage.

I recommend you do this series when each of your children turns eleven. With culture constantly banging the drum for sexual activity, you can't afford to wait until high school. If your child is already in high school, don't worry. Do this series now. It will still have real impact.

Have an Ongoing Dialogue About Sex

The Whole Sex Talk is a great way to begin the teaching process, but you need to continue talking about sex with your kids as they move through middle school and high school.

A very effective way to teach your kids how to be sexually pure is by showing them the real-world consequences of sexual sin. Don't lecture. Give brief comments about real persons they know: neighbor kids, church kids, and classmates.

"I heard that Brandy, a junior at your school, is pregnant now. Her boyfriend dumped her, and she'll have to take online classes to finish high school. Premarital sex sure changed her life."

"Bobby, one of your church friends got an STD from sex with his girlfriend. That's a big price to pay for fifteen minutes of passion."

"Did you hear about Mike and Susie? They broke up and Susie is really having a hard time with it. They were having sex and that not only hurts the relationship, it makes it very painful when you break up."

If Your Teen Has Had Sex

If your teenager is caught in sexual sin (pornography, sexting, intercourse), follow this action plan:

- He/she confesses the sin to God and asks for forgiveness.

- He apologizes in person to you, his parents, and to his siblings.

- If it was sex, he apologizes to his sexual partner and her parents. He tells the complete story, the entire truth, of his sinful behavior to you, his parents. It's important to know the extent of the sin: what happened, how long it happened, how many persons were involved.

- If he had sex, he will be tested for AIDS and STDs. This is prudent and a wake-up call.

- He will have at least six sessions with a Christian counselor who has expertise working with teenagers.

- He will tell his youth pastor what he has done and he will follow an aggressive spiritual growth plan for one year: regular attendance at church and youth group meetings, a mentor/ coach he meets with once a week, and a daily quiet time with a devotional and Bible reading.

- For at least six months, there will be restricted use of his phone, the internet, and all social media.

- No dating anyone for a minimum of eight weeks.

- All privileges, including dating, must be earned back with proven spiritual growth, a clear understanding of why he sinned sexually, solid grades, excellent behavior, and all chores done on time and without complaint.

As you can see, I believe sexual sin must be taken very seriously. If not addressed and changed, this type of sin will destroy your teenager. But with God's grace and a lot of hard work by your teenager, complete healing and restoration can happen.

Next, you need to know how to deal with your teenager's huge emotional changes.

YOUR BATTLE PLAN

1. To date, what have you told your kids about sex? If you haven't told them much, why not? What makes this so hard to do?

2. Do you believe in abstinence? If not, why not?

3. Are you willing to get *The Whole Sex Talk* video series and go through the six sessions with each of your children, beginning at age eleven? What would stop you?

4. Are you willing to teach sexual purity by using real-life examples? What would stop you?

5. Of all my action steps for a teen who has acted out sexually, which ones will be the hardest to apply? Why?

CHAPTER 23

"HELP ME WITH MY EMOTIONAL CHANGES"

DRIVEN BY OUR old friend hormones and the pressures of the age, a teenager's emotional life is often confusing and chaotic. Crudely put, teens are all over the map. They're bouncing off the walls!

What would be cause for therapy or hospitalization for adults is perfectly normal for teens. Have you heard those radio and television ads describing the problems of teenagers? A deep-voiced announcer reads a list of adolescent symptoms, each of which requires immediate hospitalization. If the hospital chain that produces these ads is right, then every teenager in the world ought to be in a rubber room! Actually, that wouldn't be a bad idea. It's just not feasible. There aren't enough hospital beds.

"My, Aren't We Moody"

Teenagers experience dramatic, rapid mood shifts. They can go from happy and carefree to depressed, withdrawn, and angry in fifteen minutes. Their moods are largely driven by circumstances. For example, your daughter talks to her boyfriend, Bobby, on the phone. She hangs up and is happy as a lark. "Bobby called and we talked. Everything's great!" Then her friend Susie calls with some negative information about Bobby. Somebody saw him talking to a new girl after school! Your daughter is furious and hurt. But then Bobby calls right back and clears the whole thing up. That girl was just asking directions to the library! Your daughter is happy again. She's back on top of the world! What a roller coaster!

Teenagers are unbelievably irritable. They are highly sensitive creatures who take offense at the slightest remark. Teasing is not appreciated, and you parents need to cut it out during these years. They have no trouble brutalizing you verbally, but you make one comment about them and they fall apart. Their emotions control their behavior. Decisions are made on emotions, not logical thinking.

Just Try Talking to a Teen

It's very difficult—just about impossible—to have a decent conversation with a teenager. Everything you say is twisted and thrown back in your face:

- "Nice day, isn't it?" "You would say that!"
- "You're going for a run?" "Duh!"
- "How was school today?" "How do you think it was?"

No matter what you say, they respond with a sarcastic, belittling comeback:

- "Whatever!"
- "Yeah, right!"

- "I don't think so."
- "You're wrong!"
- "And your point was?"

And, of course, the all-time classic: "You just don't understand!" Wouldn't you love to respond, "No, honey, I don't understand. No one has ever suffered as much as you! Unless it's me, living with you." What can you do in response to these massive emotional changes? I recommend that you move and not leave a forwarding address. (Of course not.) Here are a few practical suggestions.

Don't Get Sucked into the Volcano

There are a few main mistakes parents make when a teenager is emotionally upset (which is most of the time). First, we get sucked into the emotional intensity of the teenager. This is difficult to avoid because teens are masters at dragging us into their volcano of nasty, violent emotions.

As the teen's emotions escalate, so do yours. Pretty soon, things are out of control, and you've got a messy, emotional battle on your hands. You can't out-escalate teenagers! They can always go up another notch. It's what they do!

You've got to stay outside the volcano. If there's any hope of a conversation—some kind of connection—someone has to be the adult and maintain some composure. That would be you. You must learn how to stand in front of the volcano and listen. Don't try to shut down the volcano. You'll get fried! Don't run away from it. That's tempting, but it won't solve anything.

Listen to your teen, because in this way you can avoid getting all hot and bothered. You can keep your blood pressure within normal limits. Also, with one listener, there's a chance the volcano will calm down, and you could have a semi-normal conversation. Maybe.

Don't Be Logical

The second mistake parents make is trying to logically explain the situation. When a teen is emotionally upset, she is nowhere near the logical level, and you can't immediately bring her to that level. Men are particularly prone to use logic. Look, men, it doesn't work with our wives; what makes you think it'll work with our teenagers?

Here are some common, logical responses parents use (I've used every one of these):

- "You shouldn't feel that way."
- "Things aren't that bad."
- "You're overreacting."
- "Life ain't fair, kid."
- "Look on the bright side. Without a boyfriend/girlfriend, you'll have more time to study."

These are well-meaning attempts to reduce the intensity of your teenager's emotions and make her feel better. But they fail miserably! In fact, these logical responses make things worse. Far from feeling understood, the teen feels rejected, because her feelings have been dismissed.

Another logical response is to offer a solution. You say, "Amy, if I were you, here's what I would do." And you give her a nifty solution. Amy responds, "Wow, Dad. I hadn't thought of that! I guess my emotion was clouding my mind. You're so wise and insightful. I feel much better! Come here for a hug!" Are you kidding? No way. Amy would be angry and insulted at your solution.

When teens are emotionally upset, they don't want logic. They don't want solutions. They want to be heard. Actually, they don't want to be heard. They want out of the conversation. But they need to be heard.

Reflect, Reflect, Reflect

The only communication tool that works in conversations with teenagers is reflection (as I discussed in chapter 10). Feed back what they say, and feed back what you observe their feelings to be—which shouldn't be very difficult. No matter how outrageous or illogical or distorted they are—and they'll be all these things—let them be. They can't help it! It's a disease! They're teenagers!

As long as they aren't knowingly lying, disrespectful, or screaming . . . reflect. "Steve, you're furious and you say you're going to kill your math teacher." "Susie, you're fed up with life, and you plan to drop out of school, live in a commune, and work in a coffeehouse." "Sharon, you hate your hair, you hate your life, you hate the dog, and you hate me. You're depressed because you think you're ugly and you think you have no friends."

Don't judge what your kid says. Don't analyze it. Don't laugh at it. In fact, don't say anything original. It's too soon in the conversation—or monologue as the case may be—for that. Just reflect, giving back key words, phrases, and emotions. Your teen will try to incite you to react and suck you into the vortex. Don't bite! If you get too intense, you lose. The conversation's over, and you haven't helped. Your teen does not feel understood.

Reflection gets you into the conversation. It gets you past all the pitfalls and hazards of the first few sentences. Talking with a teen is like shooting the worst rapids you've ever seen. Only with a guide can you get through without hitting the rocks. Reflection is your guide. It is your best friend in a time of turmoil.

Reflection helps your teen feel understood. And that's pretty close to a miracle. Understanding is what he needs. He's convinced you can't understand him. You're too old and too out of it.

After you reflect, you'll get your turn to talk. And this is the only way to earn that chance. Just establish the connection and communicate the understanding first. Then, you can say what you want to say. In many cases, the teen will calm down emotionally and actually be able to hear what you say. When she's emotionally agitated, she can't listen.

When Your Teen Doesn't Want to Talk

Now, there will be plenty of times your teenager will blow up, rattle off a string of words, and stomp off. This is the machine-gun-and-run approach. You're just verbally shot to pieces. You have no chance to reflect, or even if you do reflect, he's in no mood to talk.

How do you get an upset teen to talk when she doesn't want to talk? Wait a while. Don't follow a teen in emotional overdrive down the hall. What, are you crazy? Wait thirty or forty-five minutes, maybe even longer, and then go to her and say, "When you're ready to talk about it, let me know. I'll listen." Then, immediately walk away. Don't try to force her to talk, and don't beg. If she knows you really want to talk, she'll never do it. That would be violating the teenager's code.

If you get no response, try bringing it up one more time at the end of the day. Do this one-on-one in the teen's bedroom. Typically, at this time of day most of the bipolar is gone. You ask her once, "Do you want to talk?" If she still refuses to talk, drop it. If there are some things you simply have to say about the situation, sit down, say them briefly, and get out.

Parents, Express Your Emotions

One of the ways to build a communication bridge is expressing your emotions in a calm, sincere way, directly to your teenager. Very few parents do this. Share how you feel about your job, the kind of day you had, your hopes and disappointments, and your experiences in your relationship with God. Do this one-on-one. Don't share your deepest secrets—these are for your spouse and another best friend. But tell your teen what's going on in your life and how you feel about it.

This personal sharing is good modeling for your teenager. You're teaching him or her how to express emotions. You're saying, "Here's how you do it. Watch me." Hardly any lesson will help your teen more to achieve emotional strength in his life. Plus, if you expect your teen to share, you'd better share.

Your sharing is good for your relationship with your teen. It helps create a bond between you. When you share yourself, your teen gets to know you—as a person, not just as a parent or an authority figure. It's an expression of love! It's a positive interaction. It's positive communication. For many parents, the only interactions they have with their teenagers are negative: "Get off your phone. Put those things away. Let me tell you . . ."

Share your emotions and a part of your personal life, regardless of their response. You keep initiating. You keep talking. Be brief. Don't rattle on and on. Don't expect a response. Again, try doing this at night when they're weak, tired, and more mellow. Or do it when they're in a good mood. That will happen about once a month.

Your teenager's not going to say, "Thanks for sharing. I feel like I know you better, and there's a bond between us." But that's what happened! Your teen will act bored to death. That's also part of the teen code. He'll be yawning and staring at the wall. But you go right on sharing, because it's good for both of you. You're building the bridge, and building the bridge takes time.

If you think a teen goes through a lot of emotional changes, just wait until you see the intellectual changes! Prepare yourself for a look inside the brain of a teenager. Before you read the next chapter, get to your safe place and have your emotional support animal in your lap.

YOUR BATTLE PLAN

1. Describe a recent episode when your teenager was emotionally upset. What did you do and say? What was the result?

2. What happens when you escalate with your teen? What happens when you try logic with your emotional teen?

3. Are you willing to use reflection with your emotionally upset teen? What will be difficult about reflection?

4. Do you regularly express your emotions with your teen? If not, why not? Are you willing to start expressing your emotions in a brief, one-way, I-don't-expect-a-response way?

CHAPTER 24

"HELP ME WITH MY INTELLECTUAL CHANGES"

I PARTNERED WITH NASA and the Smithsonian to explore the teenage brain. As you know, the government will fund anything. Using nanotechnology, we implanted a tiny probe in a teen's brain. For seven years, age thirteen to eighteen, the probe scanned the teen's brain and gathered mountains of data.

It wasn't hard to find a teenager to volunteer. All we had to do was offer a day with the Kardashian family, backstage passes to a Beyoncé concert, and a brand-new iPhone.

Okay, I'm making this up. The truth is, I don't need to use a brain probe. I have done extensive research on the teenage brain. I lived with four teen brains for years and I've worked with hundreds of teens in my clinical practice.

I have witnessed firsthand the incredible changes in the brains of teenagers. Teens struggle to make all sorts of intellectual adjustments. What you need to keep your sanity is a kind psychologist who can tell you what's really going on in their heads.

That's where I come in. I will now describe what goes on in the brains of teenagers and how you can help them—and yourself— through this period of intellectual upheaval.

Concrete to Abstract

There are four basic intellectual shifts that occur during the transition from teenager to adult. The first shift is from concrete thinking to abstract thinking. Concrete thinking is the thinking of a child. It is simple, literal, and present tense. Once, I told one of my girls to stop teasing her sister. I said to the girl being teased, "Your sister was just trying to get your goat." The five-year-old responded, in total sincerity, "I don't have a goat." That is the answer of a concrete thinker.

Abstract thinking is the thinking of an adult. Barring some developmental disability, all adults reach the abstract level. It is complex, figurative, and logical thinking. The abstract thinker can consider the past, the present, and the future.

A concrete statement by a parent would be: "Please do your English homework now." Simple, plain, literal, present tense. An abstract statement by a parent would be: "What will happen to you in the future if you fail English?" The future? What's the future? A concrete-thinking teen has no idea. He can't yet project his mind into the future.

Present Tense to Long Range

The second major shift is from present-tense thinking to long-range thinking. Most teens think about ten minutes ahead. They are very impulsive. They act on the spur of the moment. They'll throw together social plans at the last minute. "Mary and Bobby just called, and we want to see a movie tonight. I have to leave in five minutes. Can I go?"

Or you sit around for hours waiting for some kid to call your kid to confirm possible plans for that day. Most teens lack planning and organizing skills. They have trouble working toward tomorrow's goals, let alone next year's goals.

Idealistic to Realistic

The third shift is from idealistic, self-centered thinking to realistic other-centered thinking. Teens are idealistic dreamers. Real romantics. They think about how the world ought to be, not how it is. They fantasize about careers and the life they want to lead. Your idealistic son says, "I'll live way up in the Colorado Rocky Mountains in a cabin." You ask, "Where will you get the money to buy the land and build the cabin? How will you make a living way up there?" He has no idea. He hasn't thought about it.

Self-Centered to Other-Centered

The fourth shift is from focus on self to focus on others. Teens are maddeningly self-centered. Your teenager considers himself the center of the known universe. If they discover another universe, he'll be the center of that one too. This is annoying, but it is completely normal.

His appearance, his needs, and his life are what occupy most of his waking and sleeping hours. And he expects these personal concerns to occupy your mind. You exist to serve him and his grandiose plans. It takes years for a teenager to see the world realistically and learn how to meet the needs of others.

Now, some practical actions you can take to deal with these intellectual changes.

Forget Subtlety, Just Ask

Make specific, concrete requests when you want something done. Don't be subtle. Don't hint. Don't take anything for granted or presume. Give precise instructions. Assume your teen is still a concrete thinker. It's a pretty safe assumption.

For example: "Susie, I want you to complete all your homework and clean the living room before you may use your phone. Come to me when these jobs are done, and I'll check your work. Then you may use the phone for an hour. You must be off the phone by 9:30 p.m. Please repeat what I have said."

Allow "Friendly" Arguments

Arguments, or debates, don't do much for you. Frankly, they're a pain in the rear. But they do help teenagers in a number of ways. They give teens the chance to test your beliefs and values as they build their own. This is critical for internalizing values. Of course, you are modeling values. But you also must allow your teenagers to challenge you. They're going to attack your most cherished beliefs in such areas as:

- Spiritual truths
- Lifestyle issues
- Politics
- Abortion
- Premarital sex
- Music/entertainment

You name it, they're going to challenge it. Don't be too threatened. Allow them their opinions, no matter how far off they are from the truth. What do you do when they're attacking values you base your life on? You tell them to shut up! You tell them they're wrong! No, you don't. What do you do? You reflect. (Remember reflect?) Then you state your case calmly.

Is Abortion Wrong?

Back when I was in high school, I challenged my dad on abortion. I had always been taught that abortion was wrong, that it was killing an unborn child (which is exactly what it is). But I had heard some other, liberal, views and suddenly I wasn't so sure. My dad heard me out. He didn't try to change my mind in any direct way. He showed me what the Bible teaches about abortion, the unborn child, and the sanctity of that life, and he urged me to think and pray about it. Dad could handle being challenged, so I felt free to talk to him.

Embrace Being Challenged

If you can't handle being challenged, your teenagers won't approach you. They won't talk through issues with you. They may end up rejecting your beliefs. They will talk to others, outside the home, about the critical issues in their lives. These other persons and culture will have more influence than you in these issues. Is that what you want?

How many girls get pregnant because they dare not talk to their parents about sex, about male/female interaction, about ramifications of sexual activity, about the true meaning of love, about why you believe what you believe?

How many boys get addicted to pornography because they know they can't discuss their sexual desires and temptations with their parents?

An Open-Door Policy

Tell your teens that they're free to come to you with any topic, at any time. Nothing is off-limits! When your kids are in trouble, tempted, or have a question about life, you want them to come to you. Don't you? In so many homes, there are issues that can't be discussed: sex, discrimination, abortion, homosexuality, transgender issues, the occult, music, moral issues, spiritual questions, getting along with others and relationships . . .

Parents, listen to me. Being a teenager these days is hard.

Incredibly hard. The culture pounds away at your child every hour of every day. Thousands of messages from Satan's PR department bombard him. "If it feels good, do it." "Premarital sex is great fun and everybody's doing it." "Homosexuality is a completely normal, healthy lifestyle." "Go ahead and cheat if you can get away with it." "Morality is whatever you choose to believe." "You have unlimited, divine power inside." "There is no God." And these messages are wrapped in beautiful, seductive packages.

It's critical that you encourage your teen to talk to you about the culture's misinformation. If your kid doesn't talk to you, you'll lose her. Culture and Satan will win the war. But if you can open an honest, two-way dialogue with your child, you can correct culture's misconceptions and outright lies. You can beat culture and Satan at their deadly game. You, and your child, will take some hits. But in the end, with communication lines open and in steady use, you'll win the war.

Arguments Produce Skills

As your kids argue, they also work on their reasoning and logical thinking skills. They need to practice these skills. They need to learn how to think through issues. Don't try to prove them wrong or embarrass them. Even if they are wrong, let them talk. This is tough, I know. It's hard to bite your tongue and cry inside, when they're talking gibberish and making no sense and trampling beliefs sacred to you.

What if you pop off, and the conversation blows up and ends too soon? Wait a while, then go to the teen and try again. "I'm sorry for losing my cool. What were you saying, honey?" I know it's like taking a beating, but do it anyway.

In addition, arguing with you gives them some valuable relationship skills they'll need in life. How to assertively state their feelings and beliefs. How to disagree with others and maintain the relationship. If they don't learn these skills in discussion with you, where will they learn them? The answer is, they won't learn them. Don't tolerate disrespect or verbal abuse or any unacceptable language, but let them challenge you.

The most important area of your children's lives is their relationship with God. As teens, your children will carefully evaluate your faith and their own faith. It is vital that you guide them effectively in this spiritual evaluation process. Let me show you how to do that.

YOUR BATTLE PLAN

1. How specific and precise are you when you ask your teen to do something?

2. When you were a teenager, did you feel free to talk to your parents about any topic at any time? What topics were off limits?

3. Do you allow "friendly" arguments with your teenagers? If not, why not?

4. What topics do you refuse to discuss with your teenagers? Why are these topics so hard to discuss?

5. Are you willing to have an open-door, we-can-talk-about-any-issue-at-any-time policy with your teenagers?

CHAPTER 25

"HELP ME WITH MY SPIRITUAL CHANGES"

I'VE ALREADY MENTIONED how your kids will reject you once they move into the teenage years. But I just touched the surface of this painful issue. Now, I'm going to reveal the entire ugly truth about your teenager's rejection of you.

Open a can of Red Bull, sit in your favorite chair, and grit your teeth. This will get messy.

From your teen's point of view, you're old. Past your prime, if you ever had a prime. You're dumb, too. Incredibly dumb. Everything about you is horribly and embarrassingly outdated.

Who you are and what you stand for may have made sense in the Stone Age. But this is the twenty-first century, man! Everything is different, and poor, sad, dumb, old you just doesn't get it.

Your teens will reject you across the board:

- your clothes
- the way you talk

- the food you eat
- how you eat the food you eat
- the car you drive
- how you drive the car you drive
- the music you like
- the television shows you watch
- all your entertainment choices
- your political views
- what you spend your money on (except for the things you buy for them)
- your career
- your sense of humor (basically, you don't have one)
- your values

And if all these rejections aren't bad enough, there is one more rejection that is the most painful and frightening of all. They will reject your faith in God.

Get Ready for Rejection

There's nothing more crucial than building your teenager's faith. If there is a God—and there is—then there's nothing more essential than establishing a relationship with Him and growing in that relationship, through His Son, Jesus Christ.

Your teenagers must move from your faith to their faith. Guess how they're going to do that? They're going to question your faith. They're going to challenge your faith. They're going to pull away from your faith. They're going to compare the world's values to your values.

It's a ragged, messy process. It's supposed to be. Your teens may well reject your faith as they build their own. They'll test your faith to see if it is real to you. Here are some practical strategies to guide your teenagers to a strong faith of their own.

Be a Living, Breathing Christian

At the center of modeling is sharing your personal walk with God with your children. You need to open up and let your teenagers look inside. You need to demonstrate how your faith works every day. Everything done in life—everything—is about God and for God. You want them to learn that they exist to love, serve, and glorify God.

Passive, arm's-length modeling won't accomplish these spiritual goals. The best way to build your teen's faith is with active, involved modeling. Too often, parents teach the Bible, but they don't show their kids how it applies to their own lives. If you don't regularly connect the Bible to your life, your kids will think it's just a dry, dusty old book written for people who lived thousands of years ago. To teach them that the Bible is God's living Word for today, show your teens how it works in your life.

Children do not learn values and spiritual truth by being taught. They learn them by emulating their teachers.

Start sharing, in short bursts, your personal, daily walk with God, your spiritual victories, your spiritual defeats, how you apply what you are reading in the Bible to your life, and how you are becoming intimate with God. You don't reveal the most personal details of your life but enough to show your kids how a living, breathing, honest-to-goodness Christian operates. What you're doing is discipling your kids.

Pray with Your Teens

Pray spontaneously with your kids. Don't just pray at mealtimes or during family devotions. How do you develop an intimate relationship with someone if you talk with that person only at certain, brief, limited times? Paul teaches us to "pray without ceasing" (1 Thessalonians 5:17).

So to live out this command, you need to pray more often. Pray as issues and concerns come up. Pray for yourself, your kids, and others. Pray with your kids at home, in the car, at night before bedtime, in the kitchen before school, and on the phone. The message is: "When you have a concern, take it to God right away" (see Philippians 4:6-7).

Share Your Faith with Others

Share your Christian faith with others, and let your kids know you're doing it. In some cases, you can even do it together. The Bible urges us to share our faith with others. "Witnessing" is simply telling others what Jesus has done for us. In His last words to His disciples, Jesus said, "Go therefore and make disciples of all nations . . ." (Matthew 28:19).

Pray with your kids about those you are talking to about Jesus, and tell them how the process goes. This kind of modeling will also serve to teach your teens how to share their faith.

Family Devotions Made Easy

I've already mentioned (in chapter 13) the principal elements of successful family devotions: once a week, twenty minutes, read the Bible, make it personal, make it practical, and include prayer. I want to add some specific how-tos that will make your devotional meetings lively and effective. (Even though I'm focusing on teens in this chapter, these ideas can be used with kids of all ages.)

Always have one of your kids read the Bible passage or the devotional selection. Then briefly teach the biblical principle and apply it to your life. This kind of personal sharing is the prelude to asking your kids to apply the principle. Let's say the verse you're applying is Ephesians 4:26: "Be angry and do not sin . . ." You can say something like this: "I was very angry with Bobby earlier today. I yelled at you, son, and that's not what God wants. I'm sorry, Bobby. You still get the consequence, but I was wrong to yell."

Or if you are applying Ephesians 4:15 about speaking the truth in love, you can say: "I had a conflict with Mrs. Roberts at church. I prayed about it and went to her this past week and talked about it. With God's help, I spoke the truth in love, and I feel much better now."

Now, you can't always tell a personal story based on a portion of Scripture: "Thank you for reading the story of Cain killing Abel, Melissa. Kids, this may shock you, but I killed a man twenty-five years ago. I spent some time in the Big House, and I . . ."

Usually, though, you'll be able to personally apply the Scripture passage. If it applies to your life, it will apply to your kids' lives.

To draw your kids into the Bible passage and motivate them to respond to it, try using small groups. Divide the family into groups of two or three and give each group an application project based on the passage.

Then, after five minutes or so, each group reports to the family their findings. Your question for the groups could be as simple as: "What would you do if this situation happened in your life?" or "Tell the family about a time when you did what this verse tells us to do."

For teens, it's effective to describe specific, real-life scenarios for them to respond to in their small groups:

- You're at a party, and someone offers you a beer. What do you do?

- A friend of yours says to you, "There isn't any God." How do you respond?

- Your girlfriend asks you to cross the line sexually. What do you do? What Bible verse would you use for support?

- A classmate asks you to let her look at your test answers. How do you handle that? What would Jesus want you to do?

To stimulate participation in the application and prayer times, it is a good idea to "seed the crowd." Before the devotional meeting, ask one of your kids to speak up when you ask for input. When one family member participates, it usually breaks the ice and others will feel free to join the discussion.

Occasionally, you can share portions of videos. There are many excellent Christian materials these days, and videos typically command and hold attention. Your Christian bookstore or church library will probably carry a variety of videos. Focus on the Family has a number of superb resources in the video area.

Play Twenty Questions

Let your teenagers know they can ask you any spiritual question whenever they want to. They need to ask questions because it's one of the main ways they challenge your faith. As Dr. Howard Hendricks told one hundred of us seminary students in his Bible Study Methods class, "There are no stupid questions." Your teens will ask the same questions new Christians and spiritual seekers have been asking for centuries:

- Is Jesus Christ the only way to God and heaven?

- What about the millions of devout persons in other faiths like Islam and Judaism? Don't they have the truth too?

- How can we really know Jesus died and rose from the dead?

- Is the Bible really inerrant? I've heard some people say it has mistakes.

- What about all the people, like isolated tribes of the world, who have never heard about Jesus? Where do they go when they die?

- How could a loving God allow the terrible suffering in the world?

- How about all the hypocrites? If these persons (pastors, tel-evangelists, Christian musicians, and athletes) really knew Jesus, how could they commit such terrible sins?

On and on, the questions will come. Let them come. Expect them to come.

Encourage your teenagers to ask questions. Give the best answers possible. If you don't know the answer, say so. Tell your teen you will do some research and get back to him. Ask your teen to do a little research on some of his questions. Give him some helpful books and a few pertinent Bible passages. Ask Focus on the Family for resources.

In fact, there is one Focus on the Family book I highly recommend: *The 21 Toughest Questions Your Kids Will Ask About Christianity: And How to Answer Them Confidently* by Alex McFarland.

Church staff members are always happy to answer questions and recommend materials. Work together with your teen as she struggles to answer these critical questions about God and the Christian faith.

Keep Your Teens in Church

It frustrates me when Christian parents allow their teenagers to stop going to church. They tell me, "Well, they're old enough now to make this decision. We don't want to force them to go because it will turn them off." Wimps! That's what these parents are.

There are times to stand up and be a parent, and this is one of them. Yes, you do need to force your teens to continue to attend church. Church attendance is a nonnegotiable item. As long as they live in your home, they'll go to church and to youth meetings.

They need to learn about God. They need to worship God. They need to build relationships with other Christian kids. They need healthy, fun, and safe activities in a Christian environment. They need to know that God is important to you, and because of this, there will be no compromise in this area.

When your teens crab about going to church, tell them what my dad told me: "If there is a better place to be on Sundays than church, we'll go there."

Parents, be involved in the youth group. Do what you can to help with organization, transportation, chaperoning, and crowd control. Know the leaders and what they're teaching your teens. Talk with your teens about youth group and what they're learning.

Sometimes it is necessary to allow your teenagers to attend a youth group at another church. If a youth group is poorly run, dead as a doornail, or just a handful of kids, you may have to find another youth group for your teens. These years are too critical to let your kid languish in a subpar youth ministry. If you cannot bring about change in your church's youth group in a reasonable amount of time, bail out.

As your teens reject you and your faith (and everything else about you), they gravitate—more like run—to their friends. Let me show you how to guide them through the huge social changes they experience during these years.

YOUR BATTLE PLAN

1. Do you remember how you rejected your parents when you were a teen? How did your parents deal with your rejection?

2. Do you feel prepared to deal with your teen's rejection of your faith? What will make this rejection particularly painful?

3. Can you model a strong, healthy relationship with God? What changes do you have to make to model a successful Christian life?

4. Can you picture yourself praying spontaneously with your teens? What would stop you?

5. What will be hard about doing family devotions the way I describe?

6. Can you allow—even encourage—your teens to ask any spiritual question at any time? What will make this hard? What do you fear will happen?

7. Will you commit to keeping your teens in church as long as they live in your home? If not, why not?

CHAPTER 26

"HELP ME WITH MY SOCIAL CHANGES"

OH, THE JOY of being the parent of young children. You are the very center of their world. They deeply love you. You are their hero and they are in awe of you. You are larger than life. Your life is interesting. For them, everything you do is terribly exciting. You know everything. They want to be just like you. Their one goal in life is to be with you. They are desperate for your love. You are the wind beneath their wings.

Oh, the cold reality of being the parent of teenagers. You are rudely shoved to the back forty acres of their world. They hardly tolerate you. You are not too impressive a person, and they are embarrassed by you. You are smaller than a pigmy. Your life is boring. For them, everything you do is about as exciting as watching hair grow. You know nothing. They want to be the opposite of you. Their one goal in life is to get away from you. They are desperate—not for your love—but for your money. You are the bad smell in their nostrils.

All of a sudden, your teenagers can't be seen with you in public. Their worst nightmare is being spotted by a friend while you are in their company. It's the kiss of social death. When you ask them to go out with you to eat or shop, they cringe and say in a pleading voice: "But somebody might see me with you!"

You look in the mirror to make sure you haven't turned into some kind of hideous monster. No, you look the same. You can't even pick your teens up at school anymore. They ask you to park around the corner out of sight. They race to the car, jump in, hunch down low, and yell, "Drive!"

Their whole lives revolve around their peer group. Their peers are cool, adventurous, exciting, and so much fun to be with. They constantly think about what their peers think of them. All they want to do is talk to their friends and spend time with their friends. You aren't even considered in their social plans.

Peers on Center Stage

This not-so-subtle rejection of you is part of a massive social shift that takes place during adolescence. Your teenagers want to get as far away from you as possible and as close to their friends as they can get. You have been replaced by the peer group. Your kids move away from you and attach firmly to their friends. For the first time, peers take over the central place in the teenager's life. Parents are still important, but you now share the stage with peers.

This shift is perfectly natural and normal. It needs to happen. It is, however, a painful shift for both parents and teens. For parents, it's a loss. Your children are growing up and leaving you. It's also scary. Just when all these changes are happening to your kids, they break away from you!

For teens, the fear of rejection by peers is incredibly intense. The teenager's world is a jungle: the popularity game, the cliques, the pecking order, and the many insecurities. It is hard making and keeping friends.

The move toward the peer group is painful for both parents and teenagers, but it is absolutely critical. It is the only way for teenagers to establish their own identity and independence. Here are some things you can do to help your teenagers make this major transition in their lives.

Make Your Home a Refuge

During the teenage years, your home needs to be a place of love and acceptance. A safe retreat from the world and its pressures. A sanctuary. Even if your teens aren't around much, they need to draw strength and security from the environment at home. In war, there is the front, and there is the secure home camp behind the enemy lines. When your teenagers drag in from the fighting, their wounds need to be treated. They need rest and peace. That's your job as parents. Then, after R & R (rest and relaxation), they're ready to go back into the battle.

Be home in the evenings as much as possible. Be available, both at home and away from home, if your teens want to communicate. In person is always best, but texting or FaceTime also works.

No matter what time it is or what you're doing (unless you're making love), listen to your teens if they want to talk about something. You have to seize these moments, because they don't happen too often.

Help Your Teen Build Relationships

Do what you can to help your teenager connect with his peers. His independence and emotional health depend on developing healthy peer relationships. Do not allow your teen to withdraw and become a loner. That is not only unacceptable, it's dangerous. If your kid doesn't learn how to make friends now, it's likely he never will.

Do you know how the baby eagle is taught how to fly? One day, the adult eagle sneaks up behind the baby and kicks it out of the nest. Somewhere between the nest high on a rocky crag and the ground, that baby eagle learns how to use its wings.

The social area is another area in which you need to take assertive action. Push your teenager to be involved in Sunday school, the church youth group, school sports, and other activities populated by peers.

There are excellent parachurch organizations like Young Life, Student Venture, Youth With A Mission, Youth for Christ, and Fellowship of Christian Athletes. Solitary pursuits are okay, as long as your teenager has plenty of time with peers. If your teen is really struggling socially, you can try doing things with other families who have teens.

Respect Their Choice of Friends

Some of the kids your teenagers hang out with will turn your stomach. You'll be convinced their friends are not good enough. They're not quality choices. You want your teenagers to be friends with the best the teen world has to offer. Good, decent, moral kids who comb their hair (which is short), smile a lot, and sit on the front row in church.

I mean, why can't they be friends with the pastor's kids, the president of the youth group, the valedictorian of the high school, and the kid who went on a mission trip to a leper colony? Come on, get real. Remember, you don't choose your teenager's friends. Your teenagers choose their friends.

What you can do is to get to know their friends. Have your teenagers invite their friends over. Don't hang out with them and make yourself a pest, but find out what they're like. If you comment on a friend, you'd better be low-key and careful because if you protest and criticize too strongly, you will achieve just the opposite: You will push your child toward a less-than-acceptable companion.

If you have solid proof of a friend's acting out in a major area such as drinking, using drugs, or breaking the law, take action immediately. Tell your teen to cut that friend off, pronto. That friend will now have to earn his way back into the relationship by proving real change over time.

There are times when teenagers get connected with the wrong crowd. If you find your teen running with a bunch of lowlifes, you can't afford to do nothing and just hope for the best. Something has to be done. Scripture very powerfully warns against bad associations in unmistakable terms: "Do not be deceived: 'Bad company ruins good morals'" (1 Corinthians 15:33). If your teen stays with this kind of peer group, she will go down the tubes.

If it's a school-based peer group, remove your teen from the school and put her in another one. It's a dramatic move, but could very well save you a lifetime of grief and very possibly save your teen from ruining or even losing her life. If these undesirables are in the neighborhood or church, you can apply stiff consequences for any contact with them. You then work with your child to help her develop a new peer group.

A Rescue Story

I saw a teenage boy and his parents in therapy. He was a few months into his first year of high school, and he was in real trouble. He was hanging out with two boys and a girl who were into drinking, drugs, and sexting. Of course, he didn't think he was in real trouble.

His parents told me they were shocked at how quickly their son had changed. His grades were way down, he was skipping classes, and he barely talked to his parents and siblings. He suddenly hated going to church and had dropped his youth group friends.

At the end of the first session, I urged these parents to go through his phone and his room with a fine-tooth comb. They found clear evidence that their son was drinking, using drugs, and sexting. He had already gone too far physically with the girl in the group. He had not had intercourse with her yet, but that was being planned.

I recommended to this mom and dad that they take immediate and aggressive action to rescue their son. I said it was imperative that they get him away from these three losers. They put him in another school, cut off all contact with these three teenage "friends," and had him meet once a week with the youth pastor for Bible study and accountability.

He hated his parents for these actions, but removing him from these other kids saved him. After a few months, he was back to his old self and back with his old Christian friends.

Let Your Teenagers Go

Don't hang on to your teens, because if you do, they will not establish their independence. Also, you'll cause tremendous rebellion as they attempt to get away from you. Find ways to allow them to exercise freedom and responsibility. You have to expose your children to the culture and to the world system. They're going to have to live in it by themselves someday soon.

Know where they are, who they're with, and when they're coming home, at all times. Supervision is as vital now as it was when your children were very young. In a very few short years (though it will feel like an eternity), this primary job will be over. But at the same time, let them move away from you with confidence and a growing independence. Encourage them in this process.

So, You Want to Date

Dating is a privilege. It's a reward. It is not a right. It must be earned with impressive effort:

- good grades
- household chores being done
- good behavior at home and school
- responsibility demonstrated
- respect for parents
- good spiritual and moral life

You add dating only to a life that is spiritual, balanced, and healthy. Not a perfect life, but a very good life. If there are any slips, any poor choices, you yank dating immediately.

You don't allow single dating until sixteen years of age. I've never seen a case where under sixteen was a good idea. Young teens—despite what they think—simply aren't ready emotionally. They haven't even formed their own identity yet. You'll push your kids into sex if you allow them to date too soon. Even with good sex education—which is crucial, and is your responsibility—we are dealing with raging hormones, with a natural drive that is akin to nuclear power. Am I getting through?

Every study I've read reports that a very high percentage of middle-school kids who date will have sex before their high school graduation. The same studies found that this percentage is lowered significantly for kids whose parents make them wait until sixteen to date. Of course, we don't need to have studies to give us this information. It's common sense!

You allow your teenagers to date only Christians. And not Christians in name only. Oh, no! You'll make sure these kids definitely know Jesus Christ and are walking with Him. You'll ask these questions of potential dates:

- Are you a Christian?
- What makes you a Christian?
- Do you attend church weekly?

- Are you growing spiritually? What steps are you taking to grow spiritually?

You don't demand perfect Christians, but you want solid Christians. It's so easy for your kids to fall in love with non-Christians. It makes it more likely they'll eventually marry a non-Christian.

Plus, dating a non-Christian weakens their spiritual commitment. And don't even begin to accept your teen saying that he will win this person to the Lord. This is another area in which the stakes are extremely high. You must be diligent.

You interview all applicants, boys as well as girls. If you're married, you both sit down together to conduct the inquisition—I mean, questioning. This interview should not be held just before the date. You're not going to ask a few questions while the car is running. No way. This interview isn't even held the same day as the tentative date. This is a pre-date interview. When it's over, there may not even be a date.

You'll ask questions, and you'll get answers. You'll ask not just the spiritual questions listed above but questions in other areas. You want the would-be dater to meet the same requirements you've set for your kid: grades, chores, behavior, moral life, etc. You make sure your kids know these requirements, so they won't even try to drag some loser in front of you.

Just like a job interview, you thank the applicant for coming. Tell him you'll let him know. You tell your kid, "If any kid who wants to date you has a problem with the interview, then that kid isn't worth your time."

Do not allow your teen to get obsessed with a boy or girl. Make sure your kid has, before beginning to date, a balanced life: friends, activities, a happy, healthy connection to the home and you. You limit phone contact and time together. Dating is only a part of their lives, not all of it. School, God, church activities, family, and forming their own identity are all more important than dating.

My Time Line for Dating

Dating, in my opinion, begins in the middle-school years (sixth, seventh, and eighth grades) with group activities involving both sexes. You allow, even encourage, your twelve-, thirteen-, and fourteen-year-old kids to engage in youth group at church, youth group activities, school clubs, parties, and having friends over to the house.

These gatherings should be supervised by a responsible Christian adult every time. At this age, you do not allow unsupervised time with the opposite sex. They cannot "hang out" at the mall with a coed group. In this stage, they're just getting to know the opposite sex in a general way.

If they are attracted to someone, see that it stays very low-key. Phone time with the opposite sex is okay, but again, it should also be low-key, and not excessive. Phone contact should be limited to fifteen minutes a day.

The next stage is group dating. This can happen in ninth and tenth grades—roughly fifteen and sixteen years of age. This provides more time for your teens with the opposite sex. They can be with one member of the opposite sex, but in group situations such as youth group church meetings, youth group activities, school parties, and parties in your home or at a friend's home. Again, adult supervision is maintained at all times. You know the kids in the group, and you know the supervising adults.

In group dating, there is no touching. There is no going out alone together. There is no deep commitment in the relationship. You do not allow double dating until your teens are sixteen years old. If they double-date, they'll start out as a foursome and then split up into couples. We're not idiots, are we? At all times, we have to be one step ahead of them.

Let's say your Susie likes Timmy and vice versa. They can talk on the phone. They can text within reason; don't look over their shoulders, but supervise. They can even say, "We're going together," or "We're going out." But they see each other only in a group setting.

Timmy can come to your home, but it'll be the whole family together. You do not allow Timmy and Susie to spend time alone. Even at this level, you hold the interview with Timmy.

Single dating comes next in the progression. This is for teenagers in grades eleven and twelve (sixteen, seventeen, and eighteen years old). Just because your kid hits sixteen, he or she doesn't automatically begin single dating. In addition to the other requirements I've mentioned, your kid has to have successfully moved through the first two stages of dating. If your kid hasn't had exposure to the opposite sex in group settings, then your kid isn't ready to date one-on-one.

Also, be wary of a big age difference. I particularly don't like older boys dating younger girls. One year might be okay, but not two or more. Oh, I wonder what a nineteen-year-old man wants with a sixteen-year-old girl! Not conversation, I can tell you that. The older boy—even if he is one year older—had better be the next Billy Graham.

The last stage I call serious single dating. This is dating beyond high school. Your child is at least eighteen or nineteen years old, in college or working. This is usually the time when real intimacy can develop and a mate is chosen. Here, you still have opportunity for some input. But your child is an adult and should make her own decisions.

I am not a believer in so-called "courtship dating." By "courtship dating" I mean an arrangement in which the parents have a huge say in who their adult children date and marry. Look, once you've done your job well, they'll be fine.

There are few things in life as difficult as living with a teenager. Unless it's living with more than one teenager. These principles I've shared will enable you to survive the experience. Better yet, these action steps will improve your relationship with your teenagers and help you make a real difference in their lives.

We live in a world of screens. Technology is a major part of your teen's life. And yours. The smartphone, the internet, and social media dominate the daily experience of most teenagers.

In the next chapter I've got some practical ideas to help you help your teens manage technology.

YOUR BATTLE PLAN

1. Are your kids already pulling away from you? How does that make you feel? Are you struggling to let them reject you and attach to their peers?

2. Is your home a refuge for your teens? Are you available when they want to talk?

3. How are your teens doing in the friend department? Do they have good friends, and are you getting to know these friends?

4. Do you agree with my dating principles and time line? If not, what do you disagree with and why?

CHAPTER 27

TECHNOLOGY AND
YOUR TEEN

HAVE YOU SEEN the wildly popular television show *The Walking Dead*? It's a sci-fi/fantasy/horror show about a zombie apocalypse. The zombies, who are dead but not really dead, feed on the living. They wander around looking for regular people to kill.

Another heartwarming family drama.

I have an idea for a new television show. I call it *The Walking Phone Addicts*. It's a teenage apocalypse in which all the teenagers in the world become hopelessly addicted to their phones. My original title was *The Walking, Sitting, Driving, Eating, Lying Down, Going-to-the-Bathroom, Watching-Television, Breathing Phone Addicts*. Though accurate, it was a little long.

In this nightmare world, teenagers never look up from their phone screens. They make no eye contact with anyone, and they never speak. They only communicate with their phones through texts, photos, funny videos, emojis, and social media posts.

The teens draw all their energy, entertainment, motivation, and purpose for living from their phones. If their phones are broken or lost, the teens go into a catatonic, paralyzed state. They wander around aimlessly, sort of like . . . well, zombies.

But wait. This world is no sci-fi/fantasy. It *is* a horror show, but it is very real. I've just described the lives of most teenagers. Without their phones and other screens (video games, computers, and television), they have no lives.

Too Much Screen Time

The studies I've read show that the majority of teenagers spend at least seven hours a day on their phone and other screens. If this isn't addiction, I don't know what is.

Unlike zombies, screen-addicted teens aren't trying to kill anyone. But like zombies, they aren't living meaningful lives.

Staying in a technological trance keeps them out of the real world. They're not building real relationships. Their constant need for stimulation and entertainment prevents them from engaging in productive activity. They don't think deeply or have deep conversations about issues that matter. They are wasting time and missing opportunities to create character, spirituality, and meaningful accomplishment.

You cannot allow your teenagers to become digital communication and entertainment zombies. The price—for them and you—is way too high.

I have some simple but effective technology guidelines that will help you rescue your teens from screen addiction. But before I get to teens, a word about younger kids. This is where you will lay the groundwork. If your child is already a teen, don't worry, there's still plenty you can do.

Younger Kids and Technology

Until your children are out of elementary school, they do not need a smartphone. You do not want them accessing the internet. Not yet.

If you want your elementary-age kids to have a phone for safety and emergencies, get them a basic phone with no capability to access the internet or send photos. And they should not have any social media accounts.

The Electronic Device Era Begins

Once your kids are in middle school—sixth grade—they can earn a smartphone. It is not given to them. It is earned with good grades, good homework ethic, chores done right and on time, good behavior at school and at home, and a strong spiritual life. Helping old ladies across the street doesn't hurt, either.

As I taught in my chapters on discipline, they have to earn use of their smartphones and all other electronic devices every day.

To use their smartphone, they also must be involved in one healthy non-electronic activity: a sport, martial arts, music, dance, Boy Scouts or Girl Scouts, a job, reading . . .

When they begin tenth grade, you can allow them to have social media accounts: Facebook, Instagram, Snapchat . . . Forget Twitter. They can do Twitter when they're eighteen and an adult.

Screen Time During the Day

During the week, Monday through Friday, allow your teens one-hour of screen time per day. This one hour includes all electronic devices (smartphone, computer, television, tablet, video games), comes after school, and comes after homework and chores.

Your teens will yell and scream and whine over this one-hour limit. They'll say, "This is a concentration camp." You reply, "Yes, it is. I want you to concentrate on your homework and chores and healthy, non-electronic activities."

If they've had a good week and have earned it, they can have two and a half hours of screen time on Saturdays.

Unplug on Sunday

Sunday is a day for attending church, worshiping God, and resting. It also is a day for shutting down every smartphone and electronic device in the home. Except for the television. It's a day to watch *one* football game or other sporting event as a family.

Monitor Their Devices and Social Media Activity

Regularly check their smartphones for any inappropriate activity. You know all their passwords and will periodically check their texts, voice mails, and all social media activity.

They are not to delete anything from their phones until after you have done one of these checks.

Your teens, with straight faces and outraged attitudes, will ask you, "Don't you trust me?" You will answer immediately, "No, I don't. You're a teenager."

Phone-Free Zones

Do not allow phones or other screens during mealtimes, homework (unless the screens are for homework), or in the car.

Do not allow phones or other screens in your teens' bedrooms. Don't put a television in the room of a teen. All screens should be shut down a half hour before bedtime. Disconnect video game systems and collect phones and tablets each night before bedtime.

Model Responsible Use of Technology

Did you think I'd let you off the hook in the area of technology? No way. Make sure you demonstrate to your teens responsible, healthy use of all your screens. If you're on your phone constantly or spend way too much time on other screens, you're a hypocrite and your teens will not be impressed.

Perhaps you have remarried and are dealing with the challenges of a blended family, including in the area of technology. God wants your new family to do well, and you and your kids can do well if you follow some basic principles, which I'll address in the next chapter.

YOUR BATTLE PLAN

1. Are you spending too much time on screens? Ask your spouse or a close friend if you need to cut back on screen time.

2. Do you agree that your kids must earn use of their smartphone and all other electronic screens every day? If not, why not?

3. Are your teens spending too much time on screens each day? Are you willing to take steps to limit their screen time?

4. Of all my screen time guidelines, which ones make the most sense to you? Why? Which ones will be the hardest to implement? Why?

PART FIVE

Blended Families

CHAPTER 28

LIVING IN A BLENDER

LET ME MAKE one thing perfectly clear right up front. Sibling rivalry is normal. It's a fact of life. Get used to it. All kids fight. I laugh when I read child-rearing "experts" who believe sibling rivalry can be largely eliminated. What kind of a fairyland are they living in?

These authorities are either incredibly naive, have never lived with children, or have watched too many episodes of *Little House on the Prairie*. The very first siblings, Cain and Abel, had a pretty bad case of sibling rivalry. Hopefully, your kids won't go to the extreme of murder, but you can count on plenty of rivalry.

I can speak from personal experience. My brother, Mark, and I had a great home environment. We had terrific, godly parents who loved us and practically wrote the book on good parenting. But Mark was my brother, so I hated him. We fought like cats and dogs for years, especially during the middle-school years. There was a continual stream of verbal jousting. Everything we did became a gigantic life-or-death competition.

The main source of my bitterness toward Mark was his popularity. Mark was the undisputed king of the youth group at Christ Community Church. I was the invisible man—okay, boy. Mark had girls literally hanging on him all the time. I failed to see the attraction. It was like he had some strange power over adolescent girls. He had a string of girlfriends. There was a line of girls waiting for their chance.

I'm telling you, it was like a harem! He had tons and tons of dates. I had nothing, none, nada, zilch. Girls weren't exactly beating a path to my door. It was awfully cold living in Mark's babe-magnet shadow.

To my credit, I took all this in stride. I was actually happy for Mark. I mean, he was a great guy and deserved female attention. He was a good Christian, so maybe this was God's way of rewarding him. I prayed that he'd get as many dates as possible.

Here, I know that you know I'm kidding. My resentment burned inside. I hated him for his popularity. I prayed—out of my middle-school mentality—that he'd develop horrible bad breath and no girl would go near him.

I was able to get some revenge. I was always better at school and sports. You'd better believe I played up these two bright spots big-time. At report card time, I was in my glory. When I did well on the athletic field, I was riding high. I acted as if these academic and athletic achievements completely satisfied me and balanced things out with Don Juan. I never let on that I was jealous. But frankly, I would rather have had the chicks.

Take what I've just described between my brother and me, multiply it by 10,000, and you're close to the level of intensity in a blended family. The jealousy, the rage, the guilt games, the leftover pain from the past, the insecurities, the confused feelings, and the divided loyalties are all mixed together in one simmering pot. You've got all the ingredients for a nuclear chain reaction.

There aren't words adequate to describe the massive adjustment a blended family must undergo. It's not even close to *The Brady Bunch* television show, where all the petty squabbles were worked out in thirty minutes. It is a lot closer to World War III, with missiles and bombs and trench warfare and casualties.

Even though it is a very rough road to go down, you blended family parents can achieve success. God wants your new family to become a cohesive, integrated unit. He will be faithful to help you. I've counseled a lot of blended families, and I know you can reach the peace and stability you want. In the next chapters, I'm going to share many of the blended family strategies I've seen work in my clinical practice.

Make Your Marriage Number One

To have success in a blended family, you need a strong, healthy marriage. Your marriage is the foundation on which the kids will build their security. To survive all the challenges and get to the good stuff, you must make your marriage the most important relationship in the family.

You will face an astronomical number of adjustments, compromises, and crisis interventions. If your blended family marriage isn't a great marriage, it has no chance at all.

Because of natural feelings of guilt over a divorce, many new partners focus on the kids to make sure they're happy, and end up neglecting their new marriage. That's a bad idea.

Many children, consciously or unconsciously, want to sabotage your new relationship. For example, your biological child tries to end this marriage by forcing you to choose between her and your new marriage partner; quick, what do you do? You choose your marriage partner. If you choose your child, you have dealt your blended family a mortal blow.

In the case of the death of a parent, your child may see the deceased parent as a hero or perfect in some way. In that case, it may be very hard to accept a new mom or dad.

Do all the things necessary to keep your marriage relationship intimate and fulfilling and fun. Reread chapters 3 through 6 and follow my guidelines for a happy, close marriage.

Expect to Question Your New Marriage

Here's what will come into your mind when you run into these problems:

1. I didn't realize how defiant and nasty her kids were going to be!
2. I had no idea he would be so controlling as a parent!
3. She lets her kids get away with murder!
4. I feel helpless, incredibly frustrated, angry, and trapped!
5. Without those kids, we'd be great together!
6. His kids hate my guts . . . and some days, the feeling is mutual!

Pay attention to these next three. This is really where Satan wants you to end up:

7. Maybe we should have dated longer before getting married!
8. Life was a lot easier as a single parent!

When you think that, you know things are pretty bad!

9. Maybe getting married was a mistake!

Expect these thoughts to come, because they will. Don't be dismayed by them. They're perfectly normal. Just don't let them take root in your mind.

Let them come, let them wash through, and replace them with the truth: "God wants me in this marriage and family; it will be hard—very hard—at times, and I'll want to quit. But with God's help, we will survive and build a great marriage and family."

Now, that's the truth! Write this on a three-by-five card and carry it around with you. Repeat it to each other when things get really tough.

Expect the Worst

So many of the remarried couples I've seen have made the mistake of thinking everything would magically work out just fine in their new family. Before the marriage they tell me, "Dave, our kids get along great! They seem excited about the wedding. And we're each clicking with our partner's kids."

I say two words: "Just wait." They think I'm crazy. They're sure their blended family will be the exception. Two months after the wedding, they are back in my office crying, "Help!"

Do not entertain for a moment the fantasy that your transition will be a breeze. It won't be. It will be a painful, brutally hard adjustment for everyone involved. Even your pets will need therapy. Expect nothing less than vicious, industrial-strength sibling rivalry. It's all part of the adjustment. The rivalry between your biological and stepchildren will be nastier and last longer than the rivalry between biological siblings.

By getting married and throwing all your kids together, you shatter their carefully constructed family order. Kids base much of their security in a pecking order, a clearly defined chain of command, as well as the rituals and patterned rhythms of family life. All this is gone when the two of you get married and you all move in together. Now the kids have to start all over establishing a new system.

A further complication is the fact that, in most blended families, you have different combinations of kids living together at different times. You have this kid only on the weekends, another kid one week on and one week off, and another kid all the time.

The process of creating a stable family structure takes a lot longer due to the different schedules. Reentry, when a kid comes back to your home from another home, is a particularly chaotic and stressful time.

So expect the worst. Give the process plenty of time. On average, it takes a good three to five years to fully adjust, and this includes the extremely difficult aspect of grieving the incredible loss of the original family.

Be prepared to step in and stop sibling rivalry that gets out of hand. Don't allow physical fights to continue when it's obvious one child will get hurt. Don't allow cruel verbal abuse to pass without applying a serious consequence. When you do not witness a conflict between two kids, punish both.

Heal from Unresolved Pain

Whatever trauma ended your marriage—divorce or death of your spouse—needs to be faced and healed from. If *you* don't heal from what happened, your pain will transfer to your new partner. You don't want it to, but it will.

For example, your ex-spouse committed adultery and you haven't healed from that wound. That pain will transfer to your new spouse. You'll have trouble trusting your new partner.

If *your kids* don't heal from what happened, their pain will transfer to your new spouse. They don't want it to, but it will. All that unresolved pain has to go somewhere, and it will go to your spouse.

Your Children Have Experienced Two Traumas

The first trauma is the ending of your previous marriage. You messed up their stability and security. You didn't mean to, but you did.

They have adjusted to life with you as a single parent. They've adjusted to the visitation schedule with your ex or they've adjusted to the death of the other parent. They have their world back in some kind of balance. Believe me, they want it to stay that way!

The second trauma is your remarriage. You've gone and messed with their stability and security again by getting remarried. To a complete stranger! How dare you! The nerve! The gall!

If your new spouse has kids, it's even more of a hassle! And, it's traumatic. Your kids have to adjust all over again! Your new marriage is wonderful—for you. For your kids, it's a trauma.

How to Deal with the First Trauma

The key is to deal with the first trauma, the end of your previous marriage, *first*. When you and your kids heal from the first trauma, all that pain won't transfer to your new spouse.

As I stated before, it takes three to five years for everyone in the new family to fully adjust. If you don't heal from the first trauma, it will take a lot longer. In fact, adjustment may never happen.

Talk about your pain with your new spouse. The ending of your previous marriage is a trauma for you, too. In your Couple Talk Times (chapter 6), talk out your anger, your hurt, and your resentment. Cover, in detail, the mistakes you made and the mistakes your spouse made. Talk through what happened and forgive your ex-spouse.

If your former spouse died, you may have some lingering grief or guilt you need to deal with.

Talk about your pain with your biological children. Without trashing your ex-partner or making your deceased spouse sound perfect, be honest about what happened in that marriage. Share your feelings openly and honestly.

Do this in five- to ten-minute bursts at bedtime and other quiet moments. Mostly do it one on one. Sometimes, do it with all the kids together.

You lead the way in teaching your kids how to forgive. You're modeling forgiveness. You want your kids to forgive *you and your ex-spouse*, and this is a big step toward that.

How to Forgive Your Ex If You Are Divorced

Here are the steps that must be taken to forgive someone who has hurt you deeply. Your ex is certainly in this category.

1. Admit you have unresolved pain connected to your ex. Get out of denial. Don't act like the pain is gone.

2. Express the pain, in detail, to a person you trust. This will be your new spouse. As you talk through the key traumatic events in your previous marriage, you relive the pain. If you don't relive it, the pain remains. You don't have to relive all the painful events. God will reveal a certain number of traumatic memories that, when expressed, will cover all your trauma.

3. Write a letter to your ex that includes the painful memories you have talked through with your new spouse and how this pain has transferred to your new spouse. You will also include all the mistakes you believe you made in the old marriage. At the end of the letter, you will communicate that you are—with God's power—forgiving your ex. This letter will not be sent. It will be read to your new spouse and perhaps one close friend.

4. Stay close to God throughout these steps of forgiveness. Talk to Him in prayer often. Vent your pain with Him. Ask Him to give you the ability to forgive. You can only truly forgive and release pain with the power of God.

5. It may be necessary to use a Christian therapist to guide you and your new spouse through this process of forgiveness.

6. Involve your children in your journey of forgiveness. Let them know what you are doing and how you are doing in the process. Give them regular updates. Admit how tough these steps are and how you are relying on God and your new spouse to get through. You are showing your kids how to forgive.

You know you have unresolved pain and need to forgive if you:

- still feel bitter toward your ex
- continue to obsessively think about the old marriage and specific times your ex hurt you
- get over-the-top angry when your ex does or says something that frustrates you
- talk often to those close to you about what a jerk your ex was and still is
- do and say things to exact revenge on your ex, to pay him back for old and current wounds

Encourage your biological children to talk about their pain with their biological parent. Because you've gone first, they'll be able to do it. Healing won't occur in one conversation. Healing will occur over many conversations over many months. You may need a Christian therapist to help guide you through this process.

What you're doing, and what your kids are doing, is *grieving the loss of your previous family.* You need to do this even if the divorce was the right decision. Even if your spouse divorced you and there was nothing you could do about it. It doesn't make any difference. *A loss is a loss.* Of course, that also goes for a loss due to the death of a parent/spouse.

How to Deal with the Second Trauma

Now you can turn your attention to the second trauma, your remarriage. Don't act like your remarriage is a great thing for your biological children. It's not. It's a great thing for you. For them, it's a trauma.

Eventually, as you help them heal from this second trauma, your new marriage will become a great thing for them.

Both of you should talk through your remarriage, over and over and over, with your biological children. Just as with the first trauma, this process will occur over many conversations over many months.

Let them vent. Let them say, as long as it is with respect, exactly how they feel about your new marriage. It won't be pretty, but it will be healing. These things have to be said.

Do not allow your kids to name-call, make personal attacks on you and your new spouse, yell, or use profanity.

Let them ask questions. Let them tell you how your remarriage has messed up their lives. Let them tell you that they wish you'd never remarried. Let them tell you all the negative things about your new spouse and your new marriage.

It will be raw. It will be ugly. It will hurt you. But if you allow this kind of honesty, it will lead to healing.

With the first trauma healed from, recovering from the second trauma is easier and won't last as long. Not easy and not fast. But easier and quicker.

This chapter lays the foundation for a healthy new blended family. Let's look at more blended family strategies.

YOUR BATTLE PLAN

1. Did you have sibling rivalry when you were a kid? The answer, of course, is yes. Talk about it. How intense was it and what happened?

2. Are you making your new marriage the number one relationship in your new family? What can you do to make your marriage your first priority?

3. Which difficult thoughts have you had about your new marriage? Discuss these thoughts with your new spouse.

4. Are both of you willing to take my action steps to heal yourself and your kids from the pain of your divorce or death of a spouse? What will be the hardest part of this process?

5. Are both of you willing to take my action steps to help your kids heal from the pain of your remarriage? What will be the hardest part of this process?

CHAPTER 29

LIVING IN A BLENDER, PART TWO

THAT LAST CHAPTER was rough, wasn't it? Brutal in spots. Sorry about that. But the principles are true and will help you build a great new family. But remember, even if you've been married a long time and things have gone way downhill, there is hope. You might be starting a little late to address these issues, but the principles will work for you, too.

Here are three more blended-family principles that I've seen work, and work well.

Working Together, Create the House Rules

As a couple, develop clear behavior standards and clear rewards and consequences. Because of the complexity of a blended family, I recommend you put these house rules on paper. You and your spouse and all the children should sign.

You already know my position on rewards and consequences. If the kids choose to obey the rules, they get rewards. If they choose to disobey, they get consequences.

Do not play favorites! All the kids in the house abide by the same rules. No one gets a break or any kind of preferential treatment. Not ever.

When a Child Chooses to Disobey

Put the child on hold while you and your new spouse talk about it. Do this whether it's your biological kid or not. You two talk privately and reach a decision.

When you come out of the room, you are together. It is "our" decision. The biological parent has the final say. The stepparent has full input, but it's not his or her decision. The biological parent delivers the consequence.

Later, you can inform your ex of the disobedience and the consequence you and your new spouse decided to apply.

Biological Parent Disciplines Biological Child

Don't make the classic mistake of the stepparent disciplining a stepchild on his/her own. It's a bad idea. You will be met with terrific resentment and resistance. And frankly, that's your fault.

Biological parent disciplines biological child. Every single time.

What if you're the stepparent and a stepchild acts out and the biological parent, your spouse, isn't around? First, try to reach your spouse by phone or text. If you can't, discipline in the name of the biological parent: "I believe your father/mother would want this action to be taken."

It obviously helps if the kid's behavior is covered in your house rules: "According to the rules, here's the consequence." It's not the stepparent saying here's the consequence, it's the plan.

With a particularly difficult, obstinate stepkid, try the approach one stepmom told me about: "I am your legal guardian and the state requires me to take care of you and make decisions that are best for you. I love you, too, and care about you, but I must do what the state requires."

You may want to get a T-shirt with "Legal Guardian" and the state seal on it.

Try to Work with Your Ex

Make an attempt to work with your ex so the behavior standards are the same in each home. Go ahead and laugh now. Depending on how angry/controlling/bitter/clueless/selfish your ex is, this may fail miserably.

Chances are just about 100 percent that your ex's standards will be very different from your and your new spouse's standards regarding:

- use of their smartphones
- what they can watch on television
- what they can do on the internet and with social media
- chores, homework, bedtime
- church attendance
- diet
- what parties they can attend

The bottom line is this: Tell your kids you expect them to meet your *major* behavior standards when they're in your ex's home. Or anyone else's home.

Ignore their cries of "that's not fair." If you find out they've chosen to break a major behavior standard—with or without your ex's permission—at your ex's home, you will put consequences on them.

If you happen to have a decent relationship with your ex, after applying the consequence, call your ex and inform him or her of your decision.

Ask your ex to also apply the same consequence. If they refuse, they refuse. It's worth a try to be consistent for the sake of the child.

The Stepparent Works on the Relationship

It is vitally important that you *never* stop trying to build a relationship with your stepchildren. You keep on loving them and loving them, no matter what their response is.

They can be rejecting, critical, and mean. They can be cold and withdrawn. They can ignore you. You'll hear, "You're not my mom" or "You're not my dad." But you can hear a lot worse than that:

- "I hate you."
- "I want you to die."
- "I will spit on your grave."
- "I will break up your marriage."

They can be vicious. Whatever. Keep on loving them and trying to build a bond. Stepchildren can quit on you, but you can't quit on them. There will be consequences for verbal abuse and bad behavior, but keep on loving them.

Show Interest in Stepchildren's Interests

Do the things they want to do. If your stepson loves to fish and you hate to fish, you're fishing. If your stepdaughter loves to watch home renovation shows, you're watching home renovation shows.

Give them compliments. Go to their sports events. Go to their school programs. Go to their activities. Take these actions with no expectation of a thank-you.

Let the stepchild set the pace for the relationship. Don't push too hard. If a stepchild remains distant or hostile, give him/her space. Listen to your spouse, his/her parent, about what to do and when to do it.

It's a Long-Term Approach

By loving your stepkids, you show a deep love for your spouse, their biological parent. Your spouse will notice your efforts and love you for it.

Loving your stepkids will eventually pay off down the road. As adults, they will often warm up and appreciate how you never gave up on them.

When Your Spouse and a Stepchild Gang Up on You

What do you do when a stepchild is actively trying to undermine the marriage and it seems to be working, because your spouse is siding with his/her child against you? You need to take assertive action immediately. If you don't, your marriage will suffer serious damage and could end.

Sit down with your spouse in a series of private conversations. Share your concerns about this issue and use five or six examples. Express your feelings of hurt, anger, and betrayal. Make it clear that you believe this stepchild wants to be more important than you in the home.

Work on a strategy that will make the marriage number one and put this stepchild in her place. Ask your spouse for permission to call out this "ganging up" behavior each time it happens. You will talk to your spouse privately after each episode. After each discussion, you will ask your spouse to go to the child and admit fault and take corrective action.

Tell your spouse that you will continue to do your best to love this stepchild and build the relationship. Indicate that you will not directly confront the stepchild on this issue, because that will give the child more power. Plus, the stepchild is not the key to the solution—your spouse is the key.

If these steps do not prove effective, go with your spouse to a Christian therapist who has experience in these types of blended-family situations. If your spouse will not go, you go alone and develop a strategy.

Time Between Biological Parent and Biological Children

It's okay—actually, it's healthy—for the biological parent to spend separate times with his/her biological children. Don't try to do everything together as a blended family.

Original family rituals give children security and safety:

- Saturday morning breakfast out
- long walks
- holiday traditions

This time keeps children connected to the biological parent and helps them adjust to the new family. This way, they haven't lost everything from your previous family.

You will do things all together, and you should. The stepparent will do things with the stepchildren, and you should. But also, make regular time between biological parent and biological children.

Dealing with your ex is often a pain in the neck and other body parts. But how you manage your ex is critical to the success of your new family. I want to help you with that next.

YOUR BATTLE PLAN

1. Are you guilty of playing favorites with your biological and stepkids? If you're not sure, ask your new spouse.

2. Do you agree that the biological parent must discipline their biological children? If not, why? If you have disciplined your stepkids on your own, how has it gone?

3. Can you work with your ex on standards or is that a pipe dream? What will stop you from requiring your kids to meet your major standards when they're in your ex's house?

4. What is your relationship like with your stepchildren? What makes it difficult to build a good relationship with them? How can you do better?

5. Are you spending separate time with your biological kids? If not, why not?

CHAPTER 30

LIVING IN A BLENDER, PART THREE

I'M SURE ALL of you reading this chapter have a wonderful relationship with your ex-husband or ex-wife. It's a mature, we've-moved-on, understanding relationship. You've put aside your differences and can work well together for the sake of the kids.

Yeah, right!

A good relationship with an ex is a pretty rare commodity. What's much more common—almost the rule—is a running feud filled with bickering, competition, confrontations, and petty games.

It's no surprise that your ex is difficult. That's why he or she is your ex. While you can't control what your ex does, you can control what you do.

Here are a series of *don'ts* when it comes to your ex. I will refer to an ex-husband only for ease of communication. Your ex could, of course, be an ex-wife.

Don't Let Your Ex Jerk You Around

I talk to many clients who passively allow an ex to mistreat and manipulate them. The abuse—and it is abuse—takes many forms:

- showing up late to pick up the kids
- keeping the kids longer than scheduled
- changing plans at the last minute
- bad-mouthing you to the kids
- not contributing enough financial support
- trying to buy your kids' love
- breaking promises
- lying
- ranting and raving on the phone
- asking you to do chores or errands that he should do

This is not a complete list of bad ex behaviors. I'm sure you could add to it. There are many potential reasons for this kind of abusive behavior:

- his desire to get revenge for how you hurt him
- his desire for power and control
- his desire to "win" by alienating the kids from you
- his desire to make you miserable because he's miserable
- he's just plain nutty

Whatever the reason, the worst thing you can do is try to placate and appease your unreasonable ex. This approach emboldens him, causes your new spouse to lose respect for you, and creates turmoil and confusion for your kids.

What do you do? Slam the door, figuratively speaking, on his fingers. Every time he attempts to jerk you around, call him on it in a calm, rational, assertive way. Verbally on the phone or via text—never in person—express how you feel about his behavior. Be brief. Be blunt. And do not allow any response. If he does respond—and he will—ignore it.

When you don't respond to his rant of a response, he'll have a fit. Fine. You don't care. What you care about is keeping the respect of your new spouse and showing your kids the truth about your ex.

Don't Allow Your Ex to Ruin Your Happiness

A crazy, bitter ex wants you to be miserable. In his nutball world, you have to be punished forever for your "crimes" against him. He feels this way even if he divorced you. Crazy, right?

Show as little emotion as possible. When you do express anger and frustration, do it briefly and in a rational, controlled way.

Don't let him know he's getting to you. He's a bully and he's trying to get a reaction out of you. So don't give him a reaction. Remain cool and reasonable. Vent your guts out with your new spouse, but don't let your ex know how upset you are.

Don't Tolerate Disrespect or Verbal Assaults

The moment he launches into abusive language or raises his voice, end the interaction. Hang up the phone, stop texting, or walk away. No explanation. Just stop the communication immediately.

Once you sever the interaction, wait twenty minutes and then send a brief text: "When you can communicate in a reasonable way, let me know."

Don't Bad-Mouth Your Ex to Your Kids

Feel free to bad-mouth your ex to your new spouse and to your very close friends. This will keep you sane. But don't bad-mouth him to your kids.

No matter how tempting or how much he deserves it, don't do it. Be honest and express your feelings about him with your kids, but don't make any personal attacks.

Getting personal will put you on your ex's level and keep the revenge game going. It motivates your children to defend the other parent. Even if he's a jerk, he's still their dad and they love him.

In time, as your kids get older, they'll figure out what kind of person Dad is. They'll still love him, but they'll know who he is and his flaws. The key is to let them figure him out on their own.

Don't Fail to Have a Plan B for Visitation

If I've heard this complaint once, I've heard it a million times: "My ex promised to take the kids but at the last minute changed the plan and left me hanging."

You love your kids, but you need regular breaks from them. Plus, you do have a life and need to do things alone with your new spouse. Or just plain alone.

Always, always, always have a Plan B when your ex is scheduled to see the kids. Have a Plan B if it's only several hours or a weekend or a week. Have family, close friends, or babysitters lined up just in case your ex shafts you.

After he's changed the plan, it's a sweet moment when you can say to him: "You're selfish and I don't appreciate you breaking our deal. Too bad you'll miss being with the kids. But I have a backup plan so it's all good. I'll still get my time off." Then sever the conversation.

He'll be beyond furious because the whole point of changing the plan at the last minute was to ruin your plan. He wasn't able to do that and, even better, you don't care. These are times to treasure.

Don't Let Your Child Manipulate You

Avoid spending wars. Some ex-partners will try to buy the kids' love and loyalty. In your home, other than birthday gifts and other special situations, your child has to earn rewards.

Learn how to respond when your child threatens, "I'll go live with my dad." If the child is young and a move isn't even feasible, ignore the threat and try to get at the feelings behind it.

With an older child, you still make an attempt to help her express what's going on inside. But to take that card of manipulation out of her hands, you might say, "Well, that's a big decision. If you think and pray about it for a week, and are still serious, we'll start to talk about it. We'll look at all the factors and see what the best decision is."

Sometimes letting a kid go to your ex is a good idea. Sometimes it's not. If a child does go, it's only after long discussions and times of prayer. And she has to go for a significant period of time—six months, minimum. You don't create a revolving door. Of course, if your child moves in with your ex and you later find out that the other parent is doing something illegal or immoral, you'll have to revisit this.

YOUR BATTLE PLAN

1. What is your relationship like with your ex? What are the major issues of conflict?

2. Are you letting your ex jerk you around? If so, why? If you're being too nice and allowing abuse, how is that working for you?

3. How do you typically react when your ex disappoints, hurts, or angers you? What will be hard about keeping your cool and not letting him know you're very upset?

4. Have you bad-mouthed your ex to your kids? What have you said? Are you willing to stop this?

5. Who can you rely on to be your Plan B when your ex won't take the kids? What would keep you from asking these persons to help you?

CHAPTER 31

YOU LOSE, CRAZY WORLD!

OUR WORLD IS CRAZY. Certifiable. We live in an immoral, godless, mixed-up, Satan-driven, chaotic, me-obsessed, media-saturated, getting-worse-all-the-time world.

If you read and believe the Bible, as I do, you know the world isn't going to get any better. It's going to keep getting worse.

But you know what? That's okay. That's all right. We can't do much to change the world and its downward spiral, but we can change our kids and their future.

The world will lose, and we and our kids will win! What do I base this on? The same powerful and hopeful verse I quoted in the introduction to this book: "Train up a child in the way he should go; even when he is old he will not depart from it" (Proverbs 22:6).

What a truth! What a promise! If you raise a child the right way, he will turn out well.

I've tried to show you how to raise your children the right way.

I'm not perfect. My parenting plan isn't perfect. Frankly, my kids aren't perfect.

But God is perfect. He helped Sandy and me develop a Battle Plan that raised four healthy, amazing kids who love Him.

I am confident our Battle Plan will give you and your precious children the same results.

Do your best to follow our parenting plan. Pray a lot. God will take care of the rest.

Additional Resources

OTHER BOOKS BY DAVID CLARKE:

Kiss Me Like You Mean It: Solomon's Crazy in Love How-To Manual

Married But Lonely: Seven Steps You Can Take With or Without Your Spouse's Help, with William G. Clarke

I Don't Want a Divorce: A 90-Day Guide to Saving Your Marriage, with William G. Clarke

What to Do When He Says, "I Don't Love You Anymore": An Action Plan to Regain Confidence, Power, and Control

What Happened to Happily Ever After?: Fixing the 10 Mistakes Most Couples Make, with William G. Clarke

A Marriage After God's Own Heart

I'm Not OK and Neither Are You: The 6 Steps to Emotional Freedom

The Top 10 Most Outrageous Couples of the Bible: And How Their Stories Can Revolutionize Your Marriage, with William G. Clarke

Men Are Clams, Women Are Crowbars: The Dos and Don'ts of Getting Your Man to Open Up, with William G. Clarke

Honey, We Need to Talk: Get Honest and Intimate in 10 Essential Areas, with William G. Clarke

To schedule a seminar, order Dr. Clarke's books, set up an in-person or telephone advice session, schedule a marriage intensive, or access his speaking schedule, please contact:

www.davideclarkephd.com

1-888-516-8844

or

Marriage and Family Enrichment Center

6505 N. Himes Avenue

Tampa, FL 33614

About the Authors

David E. Clarke, Ph.D., is a Christian psychologist and speaker and the author of eleven books, including *Men Are Clams, Women Are Crowbars*; *Married But Lonely*; and *I Don't Want a Divorce*. A graduate of Dallas Theological Seminary and Western Conservative Baptist Seminary in Portland, Oregon, he has been in private practice for more than thirty years. He and his wife, Sandy, live in Tampa, Florida, and have four children and three grandchildren.

William G. Clarke, M.A., has been a marriage and family therapist for more than thirty years. He is a graduate of the University of Southern California and the California Family Study Center, where he earned his master's degree. With his wife, Kathleen, he served for nine years with Campus Crusade for Christ (now Cru). He is the founder of the Marriage and Family Enrichment Center in Tampa, Florida.